DESIGNING GROUPWORK

DESIGNING GROUPWORK

Strategies for the Heterogeneous Classroom

SECOND EDITION

ELIZABETH G. COHEN

Foreword by John I. Goodlad

Teachers College, Columbia University
New York and London

Published by Teachers College Press, 1234 Amsterdam Avenue
New York, NY 10027

Library of Congress Cataloging-in-Publication Data

Cohen, Elizabeth G., 1931–
    Designing groupwork : strategies for the heterogeneous classroom /
Elizabeth G. Cohen ; foreword by John I. Goodlad. — 2nd ed.
        p.   cm.
    Includes bibliographical references and index.
    ISBN 0-8077-3331-8
    1. Group work in education.   2. Interaction analysis in education.
    I. Title.
    LB1032.C56   1994
    371.3′95—dc20   93-40799

ISBN 0-8077-3331-8 (pbk.)

Printed on acid-free paper
Manufactured in the United States of America

01 00 99 98 97   8 7 6 5 4 3

To the Stanford School of Education graduate students
who taught me about schools

Contents

Foreword

Goals for schools—whether at local, state, or national levels—suggest to the reader an active learning process in classrooms. One conjures up visions of students exchanging viewpoints on issues, checking the validity of diverse views through reading, sharing their findings, and preparing individual and group reports. Research shows that teachers generally perceive as desirable such practices as student involvement in setting goals, student interaction in small groups, and student involvement in ongoing classroom dialogue.

Alas, research reveals teaching practices and learning opportunities that fall far short of these expectations and ideals. Teachers lecture, explain to, and question the total class and monitor seatwork most of the time, especially in secondary schools. It has been found, for example, that teachers far out-talk *all* of their students together during 150 minutes of daily talk recorded in hundreds of classrooms. During these 150 minutes, students initiated talk through unsolicited comments or questions very rarely, such initiations consuming some seven or eight minutes on the whole.

Teachers rarely question the validity of such findings. Usually, they recognize themselves in the data and become uncomfortable; some become defensive. But most teachers quickly move beyond defensiveness into questions of how to proceed differently. They know there are other ways. Indeed, many have engaged in an internal struggle brought about by the shortfall between their own perceptions of what good teaching is and daily circumstances that seem to frustrate methods other than those they most often observed when they were students. And some wince over the memories of brief forays into alternatives: total class discussions dominated by a few aggressive students, small group sessions that got out of hand, and so-called cooperative learning endeavors that exacerbated incipient racism. They have no desire to repeat those disasters.

For a long time, I have been looking for something useful to put in the heads and hands of teachers who recognize the need to go beyond the conventional ways of teaching described above—and especially those whose brief experiments with alternatives has been less than satisfying. Principles alone will not suffice. Prescriptions, devoid of understanding, undoubtedly will lead to more disasters.

Elizabeth Cohen's book, *Designing Groupwork: Strategies for the Heterogeneous Classroom* comes closer to what I have been seeking than any sources known to me. First, it is an almost ideal blend of theory and practice, with principle bridging the two and specific examples clarifying the application of these principles. Second, in addition to providing ample research support for the general concepts of groupwork introduced early on, specific research studies are then used to document the usefulness of practices derived from these concepts. Third, the illustrations range widely over ages and grades, subjects, special problems likely to be encountered, and processes to be used. Fourth, there is surprising sensitivity to the step-by-step training needs of teachers venturing into using groupwork as a way to maximize students' learning. My surprise stems not from Cohen's background (her research interests often have been guided by precisely this sensitivity) but from first hand experiences with the difficulty of being this practical while remaining true to basic principles. One is reminded once again of the practicality of good theory.

Overall, what Elizabeth Cohen succeeds in doing is to provide a technology—in the very best sense of rigorously linking a practical human endeavor with knowledge bearing on that endeavor—in a pedagogical domain that has tended to defy such rigor. Although Cohen illustrates many different uses for this technology, she makes clear at the outset that groupwork is only one way to provide students with meaningful encounters with knowledge. She views groupwork as particularly relevant to the higher order cognitive processes and to goals stressing democratic values. One is brought back to the writings of John Dewey and the enormous impact of his works on the thinking of educators. But efforts to translate this thinking into a technology have suffered either in not going beyond principles or in rigidity and prescription. As I stated earlier, Cohen manages to provide technology without falling victim to either of these two shortcoming—a rare and valuable contribution, indeed.

There is no point in my summarizing what the author has to say about each of the many themes and topics in her book. This is best left for the reader to peruse and reflect upon. For the reader interested in knowing why group approaches to student learning are useful, what is encompassed by the term "groupwork," and how to proceed with a class, not much is missing. The book has something for a wide range of readers, but clearly is intended for and will be most useful to teachers.

One theme of schooling is emerging with such importance, however, that I am impelled to say something about Cohen's treatment of it. Even though most schools are structured for purposes of reducing the heterogeneity of the student populations with which teachers must deal—through tracking and the separation of "special" students into segregated groups—the problems experienced by teachers in dealing with individual differences appear to be increasing. Part of the difficulty arises out of the fact that organizational arrangements seeking group homogeneity are crude mechanisms that create more problems than they solve. The inequities produced are such that corrective actions soon will be taken through the courts if schools and communities fail to redress them. The difficulties also grow out of the changing pupil populations in which it appears that increasing numbers of students are at the margins and at risk. We are running out of organizational and special grouping types of solutions.

Cohen effectively argues the case for groupwork in heterogeneous classes and provides useful examples of how students are drawn naturally into learning from one another, regardless of their differing levels of attainment. Indeed, these differences become assets rather than liabilities. The principles underlying groupwork presented in the early chapters come into play most effectively as she points clear directions through issues complicated by special interests and often charged with emotion and bias. Teachers who have become increasingly uncomfortable with tracking, for example, will be both encouraged and helped in learning to proceed with an appealing, defensible alternative.

Prior to receiving the manuscript of *Designing Groupwork*, I had resolved to write no more forewords or introductions to books (except for those of former students). But I knew that Elizabeth Cohen's book would reflect a lifetime of serious study and reflection on schools and classrooms, and so I accepted her invitation (albeit rather reluctantly) to read the manuscript and write the Foreword. It was a good decision because the time spent was negligible when compared with what I learned.

John I. Goodlad
May, 1986

Acknowledgments

The early work on this book was supported by the National Institute of Education, Grant No. OB-NIE-G-78-0212 (P-4).

The artist is Anne Finkelstein.

I am grateful for the careful reading and constructive criticism of Annike Bredo, Susan Rosenholtz, Theresa Perez, Rachel Lotan, Joan Benton, and my sister and favorite editor, Miriam Finkelstein.

Professor Amado Padilla provided invaluable advice on the revision of the chapter on the bilingual classroom. I would also like to acknowledge the assistance and influence of Cecilia Navarrete, who brought to me so much understanding of the exigencies of classroom life as well as insights concerning the education of the language minority student. Her work on classroom ecology provided many of the suggestions I offer in my discussion of that subject in Chapter 5.

The conceptualization of task and interaction, also included in Chapter 5, is taken from a paper prepared as a sub-contract to the Center on Organization and Restructuring of Schools at the University of Wisconsin–Madison. This paper was supported by a grant from the Office of Educational Research and Improvement (Grant No. R117Q00005-9).

Finally, I am grateful to the many classroom teachers who have worked with me in using these techniques, helping a sociologist develop useful knowledge for the practitioner.

Preface to Revised Edition

Since the initial publication of this book, cooperative learning has become a widely accepted strategy in U.S. schools. Teachers have attended a variety of workshops and have experimented in their classrooms. Instruction in the use of small cooperative groups has become a part of preservice teacher education.

Teachers in the United States are working with far more heterogeneous classrooms than ever before. Two trends have combined to bring about this change. First, more and more middle schools are moving to untracking, while at the elementary level, teachers, having become convinced that students in the lower ability groups are doing worse than they would in more heterogeneous settings, are experimenting with alternatives to ability grouping. Second, rapid changes in the nature of the U.S. school population are bringing to the classroom more students with limited English proficiency and more immigrants with a wide variety of school preparation. These two trends combined have had a fundamental impact on the challenge of teaching in today's schools.

The standard techniques of textbooks, worksheets, and large group instruction or instruction in three ability groups are simply not capable of handling the range of academic achievement and the linguistic differences found in many of today's classrooms. Traditional instruction with grade level materials leaves too many students without the resources to profit from exposure to the learning materials. Cooperative learning is widely seen as a solution to many of the problems of instruction in heterogeneous classrooms. However, cooperative learning represents a difficult technical challenge in its own right. Many teachers have given up on the technique as a result of problems they have experienced.

I have continued to work with teachers and I find that their questions, based on their practical experience with groupwork, are now different from those they asked in the early 1980s. They now ask: What should I do when some of the groups are floundering or fighting with each other? How do I prevent students from getting "burned out" on small groups? How can I help the limited English proficient student to participate within the small group? What do I do when good students complain that they are doing all the work? Or, how do I prevent wrap-up from being a boring repetition of reports from each of the groups?

This revision is based partly on my desire to answer these new questions from practitioners who are now in a very different place as a result of their experience. The revision is also based on the evolution of my own work. Since 1979 I have directed the Program for Complex Instruction at the School of Education, Stanford University. The Program staff includes Drs. Rachel Lotan and Michael Chatfield as well as eight graduate students, most of whom are experienced classroom teachers. We have engaged in a program of research, development, and evaluation of instructional strategies that enable teachers to work at a high intellectual level with heterogeneous classrooms. Complex instruction features multiple small groups, each working with a different task. Students are carefully trained for cooperation; each student plays a different role in the group.

We have worked with hundreds of elementary and middle schools in the San Francisco Bay Area and in Israel. As a result of the work of eight other centers for complex instruction located at campuses of the California State University system, these methods are employed in schools around the state. Over 15 doctoral dissertations completed by staff members have yielded a wealth of information about students working in small groups, about teachers managing classrooms with multiple groups, and about organizational support for teachers carrying out this demanding form of instruction. Throughout this edition there are references to this research as well as to the research of Rachel Lotan and myself. For example, since writing the first edition of this book, my staff and I have developed and evaluated a new treatment for status problems in the classroom, called Assigning Competence to Low Status Students. In addition to this research, I frequently refer to what we have learned, as a staff, from our practical work in creating multiple ability tasks and in staff development with teachers.

Other researchers and developers of cooperative learning have also made significant progress in developing a useful knowledge base for teachers. The time has come to bring my readers up to date on the newest developments in this field.

The first edition of the book took many of its examples from work in elementary schools with a bilingual program designed to develop higher order thinking skills. I also took many examples from my work with preservice education for secondary school teachers. Since that time, the Program for Complex Instruction has begun to work with middle schools in the process of untracking. This move to a new level of schooling has meant that the Program, under the leadership of Dr. Rachel Lotan, has had to develop extensive curricula that employ cooperative learning and that are capable of developing higher order thinking skills in very heterogeneous settings. Lotan's work has enabled me to think more deeply about what makes for good tasks for groupwork and which tasks will not prove effective. I have also been pushed to think about the role of groupwork tasks in meeting the more advanced curricular goals of the older student. This revision incorporates some of what has been learned from work with untracking middle schools. There is new material on the skills these more advanced students will need in cooperative groupwork and how to develop these skills. With particular relevance to this age group, I have included a section on cooperation and anti-social behavior.

The basic principles for designing groupwork and treating status problems have proved themselves to be practical and powerful for the many practitioners and beginning teachers who have used them. These remain much the same in the revised edition. As I have continued to work with experienced and preservice teachers using the first edition, I have gradually found which parts have proved useful to a wide variety of practitioners and which parts have not been used or have proved confusing. For example, although my early recommendations for the use of student roles have been widely adopted, teachers have experienced difficulties in defining roles and in helping students actually play those roles. I have written new materials on roles for older and younger students and on the development of roles for the classroom. In connection with status treatments, I have tried to clarify how to use the multiple ability treatment and how to avoid common pitfalls.

Years of working with teachers trying to treat status problems within small groups has led me to conclude that it is very difficult to attempt the recommended strategies without having a chance to see what a status problem looks like or to watch teachers implement these treatments in real classroom settings. As a result, I have developed a videotape to help teachers to put the words in this book into practice in their classrooms and to bridge that painful gap between theory and practice. (An order form for this videotape, "Status Treatments for the Classroom," is located at the back of this book.)

It is my hope that teachers who have been working with these challenging but promising techniques will find in this edition some of the answers they have been seeking. I also hope that preservice teachers who are reading this book in their classes will be able to avoid many of the common problems and will find that they can manage effective groupwork within their first years of teaching. Only when teachers feel confident about the inclusion of groupwork in their repertoire will students experience the joys and benefits of talking and working together.

1 Groupwork as a Strategy for Classrooms

"Why didn't they tell me when I was in teacher training that children learn by talking and working together?" asked a third-grade teacher who has tried groups at learning stations for the first time. Have you ever noticed that you learn more about concepts and ideas when you talk, explain, and argue about them with others than when you listen to a lecture or read a book? Although many of us as adults realize that this is so, very few classrooms allow students to talk together. This is a book for teachers who want to know how to make this principle of adult learning work for students of all ages. If a teacher wants to produce active learning, then groupwork, properly designed, is a powerful tool for providing simultaneous opportunities for all class members.

Small groups are not a panacea for all instructional problems. They are only one tool, useful for specific kinds of teaching goals and especially relevant for classrooms with a wide mix of academic and English language skills. The choice of groupwork as a strategy depends upon what the teacher is trying to achieve. Most teachers will want to use groups in combination with a variety of other classroom formats for different tasks.

WHAT IS GROUPWORK?

This book defines groupwork as students working together in a group small enough so that everyone can participate on a task that has been clearly assigned. Moreover, students are expected to carry out their task without direct and immediate su-

1

pervision of the teacher. Groupwork is not the same as ability grouping in which the teachers divide up the class by academic criteria so that they can instruct a more homogeneous group. It should also be distinguished from small groups that teachers compose for intensive instruction, such as the flexible grouping procedures often used in individualized reading instruction.

When teachers give students a group task and allow them to make mistakes and struggle on their own, they have delegated authority. This is a key feature of groupwork. Delegating authority in an instructional task is making students responsible for specific parts of their work; students are free to accomplish their task in the way they think best, but they are accountable to the teacher for the final product. Delegating authority does not mean that the learning process is uncontrolled; the teacher maintains control through evaluation of the final product.

In contrast to delegation of authority is the more common practice of direct supervision. The teacher exercising direct supervision tells students what their task is and how to do it. She monitors the students closely to prevent them from making mistakes and to correct any errors right away.

The question of who is in charge of the group is critical; if a teacher is in charge, regardless of the age and maturity of the students, the teacher will do more talking than the students. The teacher's evaluation of each member's performance will have far more weight than that of any other group member. If the teacher plays the role of a direct supervisor of group activity, members will talk, not to each other, but to the teacher as the authority figure who is overseeing performance. Group members will want to know what the teacher expects them to say and will be mostly interested in finding out what the teacher thinks of their performance. Even if the teacher assigns a task to the group but hovers nearby waiting to intervene at the first misstep or sign of confusion, she is not delegating authority; she is using direct supervision.

A second key feature of groupwork is that members need each other to some degree to complete the task; they cannot do it all by themselves. Students take over some of the teaching function by suggesting what other people should do, by listening to what other people are saying, and by deciding how to get the job done within the time and resource limitations set by the instructor.

Students in a group communicate about their task with each other. This may include asking questions, explaining, making suggestions, criticizing, listening, agreeing, disagreeing, or making joint decisions. Interaction may also be nonverbal, such as pointing, showing how, nodding, frowning, or smiling.

This process of group interaction is enormously interesting to students. Students who usually do anything but what they are asked to do become actively involved with their work and are held there by the action of the group. There are several reasons why this is so. Face-to-face interaction with other group members demands a response or, at least, attentive behavior. In addition, students care very much about evaluations of classmates; they do not want to let the group down by refusing to participate. Lastly, peers provide assistance so a student does not become hopelessly confused about what he or she is supposed to do. Students who are disengaged from their work in the classroom are often students who do not understand their assignments.

Although groupwork has potential for learning, talking and working together with peers is the source of a whole series of problems. Neither children nor adults necessarily know how to work successfully in the group setting. American culture, in particular, provides very few opportunities to learn group skills. These problems can be overcome with proper preparation of the task and of the students. This volume presents both problems and suggested solutions.

THE TEACHER AS EDUCATIONAL ENGINEER

Contrary to what most practitioners believe, there is nothing so practical as a good theory. Sociologists and social psychologists have useful theories and relevant research on small groups in laboratory and classroom settings. From this theory and research have come some general principles applicable to the instructor's situation. Using these principles, you can analyze your class and your goals in order to design a suitable small group format. These same general principles suggest ways to evaluate the success of the technique so that you can decide whether it works for your class, and in what way it can be improved for next time.

The advantage of providing general principles is that they can be used in any classroom from elementary to college level. The particulars can be simply adapted or engineered for differences in age of the students and in the nature of the setting. The general principles continue to guide the design. For example, the simplicity of the instructions will vary with the age of the students, as will the analysis of what skills group members already have in comparison to what they will need for the group task. It is clear that in younger groups there are potential problems of discipline and classroom management that are absent for older groups. Such differences may mean that the teacher will need to spend a longer time in preparing students, and that the groups will move much more slowly in completing their task, but principles such as delegation of authority and having the students teach each other remain the same.

USE OF RESEARCH

Most relevant for this book is the research that has applied useful theories to classrooms. In some cases, the theory and research are sufficiently strong to say with some confidence that there are specific desirable effects of groupwork on student behavior. As a professor of education who is also a research sociologist, I have directed classroom research for many years. This research has centered on team teaching, treatment of interracial status problems in the classroom, and managing groupwork in academically and linguistically heterogeneous classrooms. Many of the techniques for groupwork come from these research situations, where they have proven to be highly effective. The two elementary school settings where much of this groupwork research took place were the desegregated classroom and the bilingual classroom.

The same theories that have proved so useful at the elementary level are being applied to the middle school where researchers are evaluating their effectiveness. In the meantime, the experience of middle school teachers who have already used the results of the elementary school research suggests that the basic principles are indeed applicable to older students. These teachers are reporting the same success as those who have used the research results in the first edition of this book.

During my years of classroom research, I have always worked closely with teachers who have left the classroom for graduate work. Many of the dissertations of these teachers are the best sources of evidence in the book. It has always been these graduate students who tried to make research relevant and practical for the classroom instructor; they have coaxed me from the laboratory to the infinitely more complex and challenging world of the classroom.

As a teacher of beginning secondary school teachers, I have for many years used the first edition of this book to help them design groupwork for their own classrooms. Some of the examples in the text are taken from their projects.

HOW TRUE ARE THE PRINCIPLES?

Experienced practitioners obviously want to know how true my assertions are for their own classrooms. Will these ideas work in all settings? What are the dangers of things going wrong? Are the risks worth the gains and the extra work?

Let me be perfectly frank: I do not know for sure whether the principles hold under all conditions. But I do know of a variety of classroom conditions where the data support the propositions I have set out. What the practitioner must do is think about what is likely to happen when these principles are applied. There is no way that a set of recipes in a book will relieve the instructor of this responsibility. If it appears that nothing untoward is likely to happen, then it may well be worth the risk and the extra effort to try and accomplish certain teaching goals that cannot be reached in any other way.

2 Why Groupwork?

Groupwork is an effective technique for achieving certain kinds of intellectual and social learning goals. It is a superior technique for conceptual learning, for creative problem solving, and for increasing oral language proficiency. Socially, it will improve intergroup relations by increasing trust and friendliness. It will teach students skills for working in groups that can be transferred to many student and adult work situations. Groupwork is also a strategy for solving two common classroom problems: keeping students involved with their work, and managing instruction for students with a wide range of academic skills.

INTELLECTUAL GOALS

Groupwork can help students learn academically, as in this example of Geraldo learning about magnification.

Geraldo watches the other children as they complete their task of making a water drop lens. "What do you see?" Geraldo asks another child, as he tries to peer into the finished lens. The other child looks up and lets Geraldo look more carefully at it. Geraldo very eagerly goes back to his own lens-making task. He appears to be having trouble taping a piece of clear plastic on a white index card with a hole in the middle; he keeps getting the plastic bunched up on the tape instead of getting the tape to hold the plastic on top of the card. "Oh shoot!" Geraldo says and gets up to see what another child is doing in constructing her lens. He returns to his task only to be distracted by the child next to him. "Oooh, it gets bigger!" she exclaims. Geraldo gets up and looks at her water drop lens. He raises his eyebrows and very quickly goes back and finishes his lens. Geraldo appears to have understood what the problem was in completing the lens because he rapidly tapes it together without any further trouble. He now reaches over and takes the eye dropper from a glass filled with water. He very carefully fills it with water, centers it over his lens card and squirts one drop over the plastic where the hole is cut. Apparently satisfied with what he did he puts the excess water in the eye dropper back in the jar. He gets a piece of cloth to examine under his lens. The water slides around the plastic covering the paper and he cries out, "Oh, no!" He puts his lens down, straightens out the cloth and then carefully slides the lens on top of the cloth. He very slowly looks into his lens and shouts out, "Oooh—bad—oooh!" "What did you see?" asks one of the girls. "Look how big mine got." says Geraldo. "What are you going to write?" she asks. Geraldo looks into the lens again and says, "It gets bigger." He then takes other flat objects and places his water drop lens on top of each one. As he looks at each object with his lens, he nods his head and says, "Yep!" Talking to himself he says, "They all get bigger." He looks at the girl he has been talking with and finally asks her "Did yours get bigger too?" (Navarrete, 1980, pp. 13–14)

Geraldo has "discovered" the principle of magnification. The process has not been an easy one, and he would never have been successful without the assistance of a classmate working on the same task. Just being able to watch others at work gave him some important information. And being able to talk things over seemed to help even further. Notice that Geraldo understands the idea in such a way that he can apply it to a new setting—when he is able to understand a concept in a new setting, we know that he has a true grasp of the abstract idea.

How else could Geraldo have learned about magnification? Could he have understood it through a teacher's explanation? By reading about it? By completing some paper and pencil exercises on the subject? In order for him to understand much at all the materials and talk would have to be in English and Spanish, but Geraldo has limited reading skills in both languages. It is unlikely that he would grasp the idea in such a way that he could transfer it to new settings. In the setting where this interaction was recorded, Geraldo had access to instructions in English, Spanish, and pictographs; he also had access to Spanish-speaking as well as English-speaking classmates, and to teachers who spoke both languages. A major advantage of combining a manipulative task with a group setting is that Geraldo has a number of helpful resources, including concrete materials to represent abstract ideas and other people engaged in the same task. He can watch them; he can ask them questions; he can discuss and argue with them; he can try to explain things; and he can demonstrate ideas nonverbally with the materials. Most importantly, Geraldo is allowed to struggle on his own, to make his own mistakes. No adult rushes in to tell him what to do and to give him a verbal explanation—such assistance might well have short-circuited his discovery.

Conceptual Learning

After an instructor has introduced new concepts and has illustrated how they apply, students must obtain some active practice in using these new ideas and in applying them in various ways. This is as true for students in my graduate seminar as it was for Geraldo, a fourth grader. Traditional methods of accomplishing these goals include written papers, written exercises during class time (seatwork), and large group instruction. During question-and-answer activities teachers ask the students questions and one student at a time tries to answer, while the rest of the class listens.

There are obvious limitations to these techniques. Clearly, when recitation is used, only one student at a time gets the active practice. There is no evidence that listening to other people assimilate new concepts is the same experience as doing it for oneself. Exercises and essays are the time-honored methods of teachers everywhere. Yet low achievers and less motivated students are often reluctant to do these prescribed exercises and may complete them partially, if at all. If the teacher assigns the work during class, these students are very likely to be disengaged from their task (Berliner et al., 1978). If the teacher assigns homework, many students, especially in schools with a poor climate for learning and in classes in the lower-level tracks in high school, will fail to do it.

Even among the better-motivated high school students, essay assignments or written reports have their limitations. Understanding and assimilating new concepts and writing about them demand both cognitive processes and writing skills. Problems with writing are compounded with problems of thinking. Take, for example, the high school biology student who writes: "In the case of chlorophyll, photosynthesis will take place." Does the student understand that photosynthesis cannot take place without chlorophyll? The teacher can only guess about the student's understanding of the process. Furthermore, until the student gets back the corrected essay or exercise, there is no chance to discover confusion and error. As every busy instructor knows, the lag between students turning in a paper and receiving it back with adequate comments may be embarrassingly long.

Groupwork can be more effective than these traditional methods for gaining a proper understanding of abstract concepts. This is not to say that groupwork under all conditions will be more effective. Some basic conditions must be met for groupwork to facilitate conceptual learning:

- The learning task should require conceptual thinking rather than learning to apply a rule or memorization.
- The group must have the resources to complete the assignment successfully. These include intellectual skills, vocabulary, relevant information, and properly prepared task instructions.

Many classroom tasks simply require the student to memorize material or rules. After memorizing the rule, they must learn to recognize a problem as a place to apply the rule. Examples of such routine tasks in the early elementary years are memorizing number facts or learning to apply a rule such as: drop the final "e" before adding "ing" to a word. In contrast are the tasks of reading comprehension or understanding the principles underlying computation; these call for more conceptual thinking. In secondary school there are also many tasks requiring memorization or rule application. Students memorize certain vocabulary and facts of science or learn to solve a set of math problems that all have the same format by using an algorithm or rule. In contrast, hypothesizing about a lab experiment or analyzing sentence structures are more conceptual tasks.

There is no particular advantage in giving a group a set of routine computational examples to complete. They will respond by doing the most sensible thing—copying the answers of the student who is best and fastest at computation. The same thing will happen if you give the group a quiz to complete on facts of science or history. Contrast these examples with assigning a group the task of solving a difficult word problem in arithmetic, discovering what makes a battery in a flashlight work, interpreting a passage of literature, understanding the phototropic behavior of plants, deciding what is wrong with the grammatical construction of some sentences, role playing historical events, or learning how to plot a set of coordinates. These are all examples of conceptual tasks that can be highly effective in the group setting.

In tasks that are conceptual, students will interact in a way that assists them in understanding and applying ideas. Researchers have been able to show that group interaction has a favorable effect on understanding mathematical concepts. In bilingual classrooms where children were talking and working together on tasks using math and science concepts that demanded thinking skills, the more students were talking and working together, the higher were the average classroom gains on tests with word problems (Cohen, Lotan, & Leechor, 1989).

Exactly how does talking and working together assist conceptual learning? To answer this question, researchers listen to what students are saying to each other in the groups, code the interaction, and relate the types of interaction to gains in measured achievement. For example, Webb (1991) reviewed 17 studies of junior and senior high school groups where students were assigned math problems and told to work together. One of the most consistent findings was that the student who took the time to explain, step-by-step, how to solve a problem, was the student who gained the most from the small group experience. Putting concepts into words in the context of explaining to a peer is particularly helpful for concept attainment (Durling & Shick, 1976).

The student who does not initially understand the concept also stands to gain from the peer process. Even kindergarten children have been shown to learn very abstract concepts when placed in a group with peers who already understand the idea (Murray, 1972). More recently, Tudge (1990) found that students who tested at a lower level of cognitive development on a pretest with a very challenging mathematical balance beam task were able to make very significant gains on a post-test after working with another student who exhibited higher levels of cognitive development. Groups can help the low achieving student in still a different way. Although the student may be perfectly capable of discussing and coming to understand the conceptual goals of the task, he or she may not be able to read and understand the instructions. When groups worked with activity cards on discovery learning tasks, those students who were reading below grade level particularly benefitted by group interaction and were able to show excellent gains in understanding of mathematical concepts (Leechor, 1988).

When the groupwork assignment demands thinking and discussion and when there is no clear, right answer, everyone in the group benefits from that interaction. People of any age deal with the uncertainty of a challenging task better if they consult fellow workers or students than if they try to work by themselves. This is why the frequency of interaction on the task consistently predicts individual and group learning when groups are working on discovery problems (Cohen, 1991).

Disagreement and intellectual conflict can also be a source of conceptual learning for groups. As a result of extended arguments in small groups, sixth graders showed much better results on an achievement test and a deeper understanding of opposing perspectives than groups of students who were instructed not to argue, but to come to agreement on a controversial topic (Smith, Johnson, & Johnson, 1981). The students who engaged in conceptual conflict in this study, however, were carefully instructed as to how to conduct a good argument. In addition, students prepared pro and con arguments from their materials and then switched sides to argue the opposite point of view before coming to a synthesis. Johnson and Johnson (1992), who have worked extensively with cooperative learning groups in classrooms, see conceptual conflict resulting from controversy in the group as forcing individuals to consider new information and to gain cognitive understanding in a way that will transfer to new settings.

Exposure to different points of view in interaction helps children to examine their environment more objectively and to use perspectives other than their own.

In review, if a teacher's goal is conceptual learning, properly structured group tasks can be an important aid. However, the task must be correctly selected, and the students must have access to the necessary vocabulary and resources to achieve a required level of intellectual discourse. There is no point to a discussion that represents collective ignorance. Furthermore, there must be some way to be sure that people will listen carefully to each other, explain to each other, and provide some corrective feedback for each other. All of this is unlikely to take place by magic; the teacher has to lay the groundwork through meticulous planning, as discussed in Chapters 4 and 5.

Groupwork and Creative Problem Solving

Ed and Carl (eight and seven years old, respectively) are trying to figure out how a balance scale works:

> *Ed:* Now [let's start.]
> *Carl:* Why don't you put 4 on this side and I can put 4 on this side? [points to Ed's first peg.]
> *Ed:* I'll put 5 on that side.
> *Carl:* No.
> *Ed:* Ok, but it all should balance; we all know it, cause, see. . . . Now take them [take the blocks out]. See, balance. Now, put them back on. [He is referring to putting blocks back on the scale.] Now you leave it. [He wants Carl to leave his weights alone while he changes his.]
> *Carl:* I'll put one.
> *Ed:* Uh-huh. Hey. [It didn't balance.] I have five—1, 2, 3, 4, 5.
> *Carl:* 1, 2, 3, 4, 5. [Both count their weights on the pegs at the same time.] And let's put the rest [of the weights] on the end [the last peg].
> [Ed nonverbally complies.]
> *Ed:* I got it. [He removes block to see if it balances; and he is predicting it will balance.]
> *Carl:* Hey [it balances]. (Marquis & Cooper, 1982, Table 2)

This is a creative problem-solving task. At the beginning, neither child has the information or the basic principles required by the task. Through experimentation they gather information and stimulate each other to think about solutions to the problem. The insights and suggestions of both members are part of the success of the pair. In other words, the group is somehow greater than the sum of its parts.

When working on a problem that does not have a clear answer or a standard way to come to a solution, a group can be "smarter" than any single individual member. When members contribute ideas that stimulate the thinking of other members, the group is able to create new understandings and new representations of the problem, leading to excellent solutions and learning on the part of all members (Schwartz, Black, & Strange, 1991).

One of the serious criticisms of curriculum in today's schools is the failure to provide experiences with creative problem solving—experiences such as Ed and Carl had. The problems faced by adults in work and social settings clearly require creative problem solving, yet few adults have skills in this area. In American society, where so much emphasis is placed on individual achievement, it has to be clearly pointed out that creative problem solving is often better done by groups than by an individual working alone. For many years business consultants and educators have used the demonstrations developed by Jay Hall (1971) to teach the simple lesson that groups are superior to individuals in creative problem solving. Hall uses tasks involving problems of survival for a hypothetical group. One activity, for example, is called Lost on the Moon. The group must pull together the creative insights and knowledge of individual members to rank objects in the order of their importance for the group's survival. In these demonstrations it usually turns out that the group score on the task is superior to that of any individual in the group.

Students have much to gain from participating in creative group problem solving. They learn from each other; they are stimulated to carry out higher order thinking; and they experience an authentic intellectual pride of craft when the product is more than what any single member could create.

Developing Higher Order Thinking Skills

Closely connected with the understanding of abstract concepts and with creative problem solving is the development of thinking skills. The major curriculum commissions in social studies, science, and mathematics now place great stress on the ability to think analytically, critically, and creatively about problems in each of these subjects of study. In addition to reading and writing, the National Commission on Social Studies in the Schools (1989) recommends that observing, debating, role-play or simulations, working with statistical data, and using appropriate critical thinking skills should be an integrated part of social studies instruction. Similarly Project 2061, sponsored by the National Council on Science and Technology Education, strongly advocates less curriculum coverage and more attention to thinking skills such as analyzing information, communicating scientific ideas, and making logical arguments (American Association for the Advancement of Science, 1989). Students should be permitted and encouraged to practice these desirable skills over and over in many contexts. In the same vein, the National Council of Teachers of Mathematics (1989) sets standards for the reform of mathematics education that include discussion of mathematical ideas; making conjectures and convincing arguments; evaluating those conjectures and arguments; and developing, analyzing, and explaining procedures for computation and techniques for estimation. These calls for reform are a response to the judgement that knowledge acquired by rote memory is insufficient for the challenges of modern social problems and modern technology. Future citizens should not only know how to think and how to deal with very uncertain problems, but they should also know how to communicate and share those thinking processes with others.

The group situation is ideal for the development of thinking skills. Cooperative groups provide learners with the opportunity to practice generating causes and effects, hypothesizing, categorizing, deciding, inducing, and problem-solving (Solomon, Davidson, & Solomon, 1992). In comparing cooperative learning with competitive and individualistic learning, the Johnsons (1992) found that there were more frequent experiences of discovery and use of higher level reasoning strategies in the group setting. These two experts in cooperative learning summarize their extensive research on why cooperation aids in the development of higher level cognition and the ability to communicate thinking: discussion within the group promotes more frequent oral summarizing, explaining, and elaborating what one knows; cooperative learning promotes greater ability to take the perspective of others (an important thinking skill in social studies); in the group setting, one's thinking is monitored by others and has the benefit of both the input of other people's thinking and their critical feedback.

Group interaction is not only the most effective but the most practical way of achieving these goals. Standards such as those of current math educators simply cannot be accomplished by having students work by themselves—there is simply too much for the teachers to "teach" (Bassarear & Davidson, 1992). These two math educators feel that students can often address other students' questions more effectively than the teacher. In addition, discussion often captures various students' misconceptions that the teacher may never uncover.

Information, Retention, and Improvement of Basic Skills

Cooperative learning is also an effective strategy in helping students understand and retain information as well as in improving their basic skills. Many researchers have compared the effectiveness of cooperative groups to traditional methods of instruction in teaching students skills that are measured on multiple choice tests. In general, there have been some very significant positive effects on achievement that occur as a result of cooperative learning (Johnson, Johnson, & Maruyama, 1983; Johnson, Maruyama, Johnson, Nelson, & Skon, 1981). In some studies, however, cooperative learning was associated with results that were merely as good as those with more traditional forms of instruction and not necessarily superior (Davidson, 1985; Newmann & Thompson, 1987).

The important message that this literature on effectiveness has for the classroom teacher is that there are clearly some conditions under which cooperative learning is more effective than traditional methods of instruction. Whether or not groups are more effective than other methods of instruction depends on factors such as the choice of task, whether or not students are willing to help each other, and what motivations members have to become engaged in the group activity. Simply telling students to get in a group and carry out familiar classroom tasks designed to improve basic skills is not sufficient to insure learning gains.

Groupwork and Oral Language Proficiency

Cooperative tasks are an excellent tool for still one more cognitive teaching goal—the learning of language and the improvement of oral communication. In any language learning setting, in bilingual classrooms, or for students of any age who need to improve skills in oral communication, active practice is essential. Recitation and drill are of limited effectiveness, producing much less active practice than a group exercise where students talk with each other.

Specialists in language learning argue, for example, that there is too much reliance on pattern drills in the English as a Second Language approach. Children learn language by using it in a more natural, meaningful context. If the instructor of the classroom where children need to increase oral proficiency in English sets up a series of tasks that stimulate children to talk to each other, using new vocabulary associated with an interesting task, the possibilities for active language learning can be greatly enhanced.

In a review of research on second language acquisition in cooperative learning, Mary McGroarty (1989) finds evidence that students gain both in comprehension and production of the second language. She finds that tasks used in cooperative learning foster many different types of verbal exchange. There are more possibilities for fluent speakers to tailor speech and interactions so that they can be understood by the less proficient speaker. Even when all the students in a group lack fluency in English, the students will correct each other and attempt to fill in the gaps of their understanding by repairing and rephrasing what their partners say in order to come to agreement.

The very same proposition applies to the teaching of foreign languages in secondary school and to speech classes where the instructor is trying to increase skills in oral communication. Compare the traditional approach of having one student stand up and make a presentation to the class with setting up small groups where each member is responsible for communicating a key part of the task. If the group must understand what each member has to say in order to accomplish the goal, they will ask questions and force the presenter to be a clear communicator. The group method will provide far more active and relevant practice than having students take turns in making a speech to the whole class.

SOCIAL GOALS

Social research has gathered impressive evidence to show that when people work together for group goals, there are a number of desirable effects on people's feelings for one another. When groups engage in cooperative tasks, they are more likely to form friendly ties, to trust each other, and to influence each other than when the task stimulates competition among members (Deutsch, 1968). Studies of cooperative learning in classrooms show similar results. When students were taken out of class and given a group task, those who came from classes using cooperative learning showed far more helpful and cooperative behavior—and much reduced negative or competitive behavior—than those coming from classrooms where only whole class instruction was in use (Sharan et al., 1984).

Positive Intergroup Relations

Cooperative groups and teams are particularly beneficial in developing harmonious interracial relations in desegregated classrooms. Slavin (1983) reviewed fourteen cooperative classroom experiments whose groups were ethnically and/or racially mixed. In eleven of these studies there were significantly more friendship choices across racial and ethnic lines among those students who had worked in cooperative, interracial groups than among students who had not had this opportunity. Particularly striking are the results of Slavin's team method (1983, p. 13), where interracial groups are given an overall score achieved by combining test scores of individual members of the team. In his book on cooperative learning, Slavin concludes that it is high quality positive interpersonal interaction that leads to interpersonal attraction; through interaction individuals perceive underlying similarities across racial lines (Slavin, 1983, Chapter 4). Cooperative goals or group rewards help to produce this deeper level of interaction, interaction that is not usually available in desegregated classrooms.

Sharan and his colleagues have examined how members of different ethnic groups treat each other while working together on a cooperative goal. Their comparison of techniques of cooperative learning such as Group Investigation with traditional whole class instruction shows that cooperative learning produces more cross-ethnic cooperation and less negative and competitive behavior between members of different ethnic groups (Sharan et al., 1984, pp. 73–103; Sharan & Shachar, 1988).

It is true that an instructor is more likely to produce positive intergroup relations with cooperative groups than with a competitive or individualized reward system. Yet even under cooperative conditions, groups can fail to "mesh" and to achieve a unified "we" feeling. Interpersonal relations can at times be the opposite of harmonious; certain individuals can completely dominate the interaction of the group. To obtain the benefits of cooperation, it is necessary to prepare the students for the cooperative experience. Researchers and educators who work with cooperative classroom groups (including Sharan) have developed ways to train students for the experience of groupwork.

Socializing Students for Adult Roles

Of all the educators who have written about the favorable effects of small groups in the classroom, only the Sharans (Sharan & Sharan, 1976) point out that when the teacher delegates authority to a student group and allows that group to make decisions as to how it will proceed on its task, there is a special socializing effect. The Sharans argue that having students experience making decisions on their own rather than telling them exactly what to do will have a desirable political socializing effect on them. They will have more of a sense of control of their own environment, and they will learn how to be active citizens (in a collective rather than in an individualistic sense). This constitutes an antidote to methods of classroom organization where the teacher does all the directing and tells others what to do while the student plays a passive role.

Another way in which groups socialize students for adult roles is by teaching them how to carry on a rational, organized discussion and how to plan and carry out a task as a result of that discussion. This is a set of skills that adults frequently lack. They do not know how to listen to others or how to work with other people's ideas; they are often more concerned with dominating the discourse than with participating. In so many aspects of adult work and organizational life these skills are critical, yet we rarely teach them in formal education.

The Sharans attribute both the idea of an active decision-making role for students and the importance of being able to think for oneself and being able to exchange ideas and opinions freely with others to Dewey (Sharan & Sharan, 1992, pp. 2–6). Dewey felt that schooling "should embody in its very procedures the process and goals of democratic society" (Sharan & Sharan, 1992, p. 4). In this way, students will prepare for their role as adult citizens in a democracy.

SOLVING COMMON CLASSROOM PROBLEMS

From the teacher's point of view, groupwork solves two common discipline problems. It helps with the problem of the low achieving student who is often found doing anything but what he or she is supposed to be doing. Moreover, it helps to solve the problem of what the rest of the class should be doing while the teacher works intensively with one group. The most typical strategy is to have the rest of the students working with pencil and paper at their seats. However, this produces all kinds of discipline problems. If the rest of the class has been trained to work independently in groups, teachers will be free to devote their attention to giving direct instruction to one small group.

Increasing Time on Task

Research has led many schools to become concerned with how much time children are actually spending on learning tasks. The issue is important because of the frequently observed relationship between the amount of time children spend in classroom learning activities and their score on achievement tests.

One of the major ways that children lose time on task is through the use of seatwork techniques. The Beginning Teacher Evaluation Study, a monumental work of classroom observation and achievement testing, revealed that on the average students observed in Grades 2 and 5, spent at least 60 percent of their time in seatwork (Berliner et al., 1978). For over half the time during reading and mathematics, the students observed worked on their own, with no instructional guidance. The amount of time children were on task in these self-paced settings was markedly lower than in other classroom settings.

This means that students are often doing something other than their assigned work when they are left to their own devices—and the students observed in the *Beginning Teacher* study were the students who needed to work hard; they were achieving in the 30–60th percentile on standardized tests. Furthermore, regardless of the achievement level of the students in the fall, this study found strong relationships between time on task and achievement test scores in the spring.

Studies of seatwork consistently find this method of instruction has higher rates of disengagement than whole class instruction. Although seatwork can be supervised effectively, this is frequently not the case. Students often find seatwork assignments meaningless and confusing; they may lack the resources to complete the task properly. In a study of Title I schools (Anderson, 1982), young children were interviewed about what they thought they were doing during seatwork. Many did not understand the purpose of the assignment; "getting it done" was what many students, both high and low achievers, seemed to see as the main reason for doing the task. Of these students, about 30 percent (all of whom were low achievers) apparently did not expect their assignments to make any sense.

Choosing a method of classroom organization that leaves the student who rarely succeeds in schoolwork quite alone may indeed be the root cause of the observed disengagement on the part of low achieving students in seatwork settings. These students are receiving very little information on the purpose of their assignment, on how to complete it successfully, on how they are doing, or on how they could be more successful. The tasks themselves are rarely sufficiently interesting to hold the students' attention. Students drift off task simply because there is nothing to compel them to stay with it except the teacher's command to "get the job done."

Groupwork will usually produce more active, engaged task-oriented behavior than seatwork. The interactive student situation provides more feedback to the struggling student. Interaction provides more opportunities for active rehearsal of new concepts for students of all achievement levels. Students who cannot read or do not understand the instructions can receive help from their peers (as in the case of Geraldo). If the group is held accountable for its work, there will be strong group forces that will prevent members from drifting off task. Finally, peer interaction, in and of itself, is enormously engaging and interesting to students. All these factors help to account for research findings such as that of Ahmadjian (1980) who studied low achieving students in fifth and sixth grade classrooms. She found dramatically increased rates of time on task for these students doing groupwork as compared to seatwork.

Managing Academic Heterogeneity

Many teachers are faced with students who possess a wide range of academic and linguistic skills in their classes. This is particularly characteristic of schools serving students from lower socioeconomic backgrounds. In many areas of the United States there are classrooms with students who have wide variability in English proficiency. As every teacher knows, this creates tremendous problems. What level of instruction is appropriate? Should students who lack prerequisite academic and English skills be given the same assignment as everyone else, even though they are bound to fail? What should the teacher do with the students who are operating on grade level while giving much-needed attention to students who are so far behind?

The most commonly attempted methods of solving these dilemmas are ability grouping and individualized seatwork. But there is no evidence that putting low achieving students into a homogeneous ability group is effective (Slavin, 1987). On the contrary, low achieving students clearly benefit from heterogeneous groups and classrooms where there are more academic resources available to them (Dar & Resh, 1986; Kerckhoff, 1986). And the problems with giving seatwork assignments to students who are operating below grade level have already been emphasized.

An alternative strategy is the use of heterogeneous groups that are trained to use their members as resources. If two students in the group can read, then they can read the instructions to others. If the group problem requires subtraction, and only one student knows how to do subtraction, then that student may be able to show the others how to do it. If several students speak only Spanish and one student is fully bilingual, then the bilingual student can serve as interpreter between the English and Spanish speaking students.

This format allows the teacher to challenge the students intellectually rather than to teach to the lowest common denominator. If each group member is required to turn out a product demonstrating understanding but is allowed to use resources in the group to achieve that understanding, the student with weak academic skills will not sit back and go along with the group. If the task is challenging and interesting, he or she will become actively engaged and will demand assistance and explanation. For students more advanced in academic skills, the act of explaining to others represents one of the first ways to solidify their own learning (Webb, 1983).

In review, if students are properly prepared, heterogeneous groups can represent a solution to one of the most persistent problems of classroom teaching. If students are able to use each

other as resources, everyone can be exposed to grade-level curriculum and even more challenging material. Lack of skills in
reading, writing, and computation need not bar students from
exposure to lessons requiring conceptualization. At the same
time, these students can develop their basic skills with assistance
from their classmates.

3 The Dilemma of Groupwork

Common problems in groupwork can be illustrated by a visit to a hypothetical classroom, in this case that of Ms. Todd, who is making her first attempt at using groupwork in her class. Ms. Todd has decided that she has been doing too much of the talking in class and that students should have the opportunity for more participation. She has given her fifth grade class a group assignment in social studies based on a chapter from the textbook along with the comprehension questions provided in the teacher's manual. The class has supposedly already read this chapter. Each group has been told that they are expected to answer the questions as a group. At the end of the period each group is to hand in one set of answers that represents the group's opinion. Ms. Todd was afraid that if she tried to compose the groups, the students would be upset at being separated from their friends. Therefore she has told them that they must find a group of four with whom they would like to work.

We look in on the classroom ten minutes into the period and find the work under way: There is a constructive buzz of voices as students bend to their task. Everything appears to be going very well indeed, although as we look around we realize that the groups have segregated themselves so that they are either all boy or all girl. Wait a minute! What is going on in the group by the window? As we quietly move nearer we can see that two of the four students have their heads together over the book. One has the answer paper and the other is leafing through the chapter looking for the answer. The other two members of the group, however, are not working on this task at all. One seems to be finishing a math assignment, and the other is gazing dreamily out the window.

And look at that other group in the back of the room! Did you hear what they said? One girl just told the other that she didn't have time to read the chapter, so she won't be much help. Another is saying to the group, "Look, Susanna is the only one who gets A's in social studies, so we should only put down what she thinks. Susanna, you tell us the answers, and I'll write them down for you."

In a third group of boys over by the door, Rick Williams is acting like a regular Mr. Take-Charge. He is telling everyone where to look things up, and then when they come up with an answer, he always thinks he has a better idea. What's worse— even when his ideas are clearly wrong, the group goes along with him.

There are just three African-American students in this oth- erwise all-white classroom (the school is part of a small voluntary desegregation program). How are they doing in the groupwork scene? Look, two of them are not saying very much in their groups. They have the book open and look interested, but no one in the group is paying any attention to them.

And how is poor little Annie doing? No one chose Annie as a group member because she doesn't have any friends in the class. Ms. Todd whispers to us that she had to "persuade" one of the groups to accept Annie as a member and that it was em- barrassing. Annie, at the moment we observe, has her head on her arms; her eyes are closed.

Now things are getting a little out of hand. In still another group two boys are just about to come to blows over what is the right answer. They don't seem so concerned over social studies as they are over who is going to be boss. These two are friends, but they fight all the time. At least they are arguing over the assignment which is better than one of the other groups of boys currently engaged in an arm-wrestling contest. That is not too surprising, considering that Jimmy is the ringleader: Jimmy can only read at the third-grade level and just hates social studies.

"Let's have a little order in here!" pleads Ms. Todd, who has been moving around the room and has seen what is going on. "Five more minutes," she calls out—even though the period is only half over. We decide we had better leave. Ms. Todd looks uncomfortable with having visitors and she is not pleased with what is happening.

Why were the results of Ms. Todd's experiment so dismaying? This classroom scene raises many issues about what goes on inside small groups. Why do the students allow one member of the group to do all the work and make all the decisions? It makes some sense in Susanna's case, because she really is a top notch student, but look at Rick's group. They are going along with Rick's ideas even when they must know he is wrong—he just talks more loudly than the others. In the cases of Rick and Jimmy (the classroom troublemaker and the school-yard hero), the two students who are arguing foolishly just to see whose opinion will carry the day, and unpopular little Annie, it is almost as if the pecking order of student play and friendship groups has invaded the classroom groups. And why aren't the students nicer to each other? Why aren't they aware of how those two African-American students must feel about having no chance to talk? And why don't they see that Annie is on the verge of tears?

One thing is clear: The teacher who has no more tools for the planning of groupwork than an initial attraction to an idea of groupwork as a democratic and creative setting for learning is likely to run into trouble in trying out the new methods. Although the results are unlikely to be as consistently disappointing as in Ms. Todd's class, careful observation of any class working under her form of grouping and task instruction will reveal patterns of undesirable domination on the part of some students and nonparticipation and withdrawal on the part of others. In addition, there appear to be both disciplinary and motivational problems that are not characteristic of Ms. Todd's class when she uses her more traditional methods of whole class presentation or well-supervised seatwork.

Some of these disciplinary and motivational problems are closely related to our initial observations of domination and lack of participation. Some are related to Ms. Todd's failure to select and define a more suitable task for the groupwork setting and her failure to prepare the students in the skills they will need for groupwork. This chapter focuses on the problems of unequal participation and undesirable domination of groups by certain students.

Let us imagine that Ms. Todd persists beyond the first trial and in her second attempt tries to compose groups so that students of more similar abilities are placed together. She reasons that one student who gets much better grades won't take over and do all the work. Furthermore, this arrangement has the added advantage of separating friends who play rather than work, spares her the problem of Annie the social isolate, and desegregates the sexes.

As she walks around the room and listens carefully to what is happening in each group, she finds that although the discipline problem is much improved, in most of her groups one student is doing far more talking and deciding than anyone else, and at least one student is saying practically nothing. Again two of the three African-American students are quiet members of their respective groups. In at least one of the groups she observes, there is a real struggle going on as to whose opinion will be adopted by the group. Their talk is not an intellectual discussion about the meaning of the chapter but an interpersonal conflict over who is going to be the leader of the group.

What is the matter? Are the students just too immature to work in groups? The problem is not one of immaturity: Adults working in small groups will also exhibit problems of dominance—they will struggle over leadership in a group and will participate unequally.

BEHAVIOR OF TASK-ORIENTED GROUPS

Small task groups tend to develop hierarchies where some members are more active and influential than others. This is a *status ordering*—an agreed-upon social ranking where everyone feels it is better to have a high rank within the status order than a low rank. Group members who have high rank are seen as more competent and as having done more to guide and lead the group.

In the more than 100 four-person groups of schoolchildren

I have studied, I have rarely found that each person contributes one-fourth of the speeches on the task. Even among a group of adults who do not know each other and who have been selected for a laboratory study on the basis that they are all male, nineteen or twenty years old, and white, inequalities in interaction and a status order will emerge. After the task is completed, group members are likely to agree that the person who has done the most talking has made the most important contribution to the task and has had the best ideas, while the person who was relatively quiet is seen as having made the least important contribution and is felt to have contributed few good ideas (Berger, Conner, & McKeown, 1974).

The very same problem occurs in groups of students who have been well-prepared for cooperative learning. These students may treat each other with civility, but still exhibit unequal participation and all the other signs of a status order among the members of the group. Among the developers of methods of cooperative learning, there is often a confusion between what I am calling a status problem that is based on different expectations for competence and a problem of unfriendliness and distrust. A group can be very friendly and trusting and still exhibit a sharp status order, with some members perceived as much more competent than others.

Expert Status

If dominance and inequality emerge in groups with members who are equal in status, then we should not be surprised to find these patterns in classroom groups where students have known each other on an intensive basis in what is often a competitive setting. In the classroom it is impossible to compose groups where all members have equal status. Students generally have an idea of the relative competence of each of their classmates in important subjects like reading and math acquired from listening to their classmates perform, from hearing the teacher's evaluation of that performance, and from finding out each other's marks and grades. They usually can, if asked, place each of their classmates in a rank order of competence in reading and math. This ranking forms an *academic status order* in the classroom.

Students who have high standing in an academic subject are very likely to dominate a group given a task from that subject area—recall Susanna's group in Ms. Todd's class. Susanna was viewed as a very successful student in social studies. People who are seen as knowing more about the specific topic of the group task are very likely to be highly influential in the group. In other words, they are high status individuals. Expert status is an important idea for the designer of groupwork. If you assign a group a task from regular academic work, the student who is seen as getting the best grades in that subject is likely to dominate the group. Even if you think you have picked group members of similar ability, the students are likely to make very fine distinctions about who is the best student in the small group.

As a teacher you may decide that there is nothing undesirable about experts dominating their groups, as long as they are on the right track on this particular assignment. If they are not, the group may miss the point of the assignment because members are unwilling to argue with the expert. Also, students who feel as if they are distinctly less expert within the group may sit back and play a very passive role, learning little from the experience.

Academic Status

Now suppose Ms. Todd does not pick a social studies task from the textbook. Suppose she asks her students to play a simple board game called Shoot the Moon. On the board are many different paths to the moon. Depending on which square the playing piece lands on, the group stands to win or lose the number of points printed in each square on the board. A roll of a die determines how many spaces the playing piece advances. The group has only fourteen turns to reach the goal in their rocket ship. For each turn, they must come to agreement as to which way to proceed on the board.

Shoot the Moon is a game requiring no academic skills. There is no rational connection between reading skills and the ability to play Shoot the Moon. Yet the student who is seen as best in reading is very likely to dominate the discussion. And the student who is seen as poor in reading is very likely to be relatively inactive in this game. Reading ability, as perceived by others, is an important kind of academic status. And academic status has the power to spread to new tasks where there is no rational connection between the abilities required by the task and the academic skill making up the status order.

Rosenholtz (1985) demonstrated the power of reading ability to affect the status order in classroom groups playing Shoot the Moon. After she asked fifth- and sixth-grade children to rank each other on how good they were in reading, she composed groups with two classmates who were seen as more able in reading and two who were seen as less able. Those perceived as better readers were more active and influential compared to those seen as less able in reading. Thus reading ability, a kind of academic status, had the power to spread to a task where reading was irrelevant.

Children (and some teachers) see reading ability as an index of something more general than a specific, relatively mechanical skill. Reading ability is used as an index of how smart a student is. Thus good readers expect to be good at a wide range of school tasks, and poor readers expect to do poorly at just as wide a range of schoolwork.

Rank on reading ability is evidently public knowledge in many elementary classrooms. In most of the classrooms studied by Rosenholtz and Wilson (1980) the students were able to rank order each other on reading ability with a high level of agreement. Furthermore, the teacher's ranking was in agreement with the student's ranking. This means that if you are a poor reader, it is not only you who expect to do poorly— all your classmates expect you to do poorly as well! It is an unenviable status, particularly when one thinks of how many hours a day you are imprisoned in a situation where no one expects you to perform well. Even in the higher grades where reading is no longer a regular subject of study, students will still show considerable agreement on who in the class is best in schoolwork and who has the most trouble with schoolwork (Hoffman & Cohen, 1972). Just as in the Rosenholtz study described above, Hoffman found that those students who were seen as better in schoolwork tended to be more dominant on a game requiring no academic skill in comparison to those who were seen as less able in schoolwork.

What happens when small groups of students work on tasks that require academic skills *as well as* many other skills such as spatial ability or dramatic ability? In this case the good reader or the student who gets the best grades in math or social studies is expert on some part of the task, but is less expert on other parts. If this were a rational world, we would expect to see different students acting as experts for different parts of the task.

This is *not,* however, what happens. Studies of classroom groups involved in tasks requiring many different abilities reveal that those students who are perceived to be good at math or science (Cohen, 1984) or good at social studies (Bower, 1990) do much more of the talking about all phases of the task than the other students. Those students who are perceived as weak in the relevant subject matter say very little and when they do participate, they tend to be ignored.

Perhaps, you may argue, these students are listened to because they really are high ability individuals who do well on a variety of intellectual tasks. Dembo and McAuliffe (1987) demonstrated clearly that what is going on here is due to the perceptions of "high ability" rather than to some actual difference in ability. They used a bogus test of problem solving to label some students publicly as "high ability." The students so labeled also turned out to be more active and influential in small groups working cooperatively than those labeled as "average" on the bogus test. Thus it is clear that perceived academic or intellectual ability, whether it is actually relevant to the task or not, has the power to affect both participation and influence in small groups of students.

Peer Status

Returning to Ms. Todd's class for a moment, why did we see some children who had a high social standing among their peers (like Rick and Jimmy) dominate in their groups even though they were not good students? And why was Annie, who had no

friends, so inactive in her group? Students create their own status orders as they play and interact with each other at school
and outside of school. Those who have a higher social standing
have high *peer status* and are likely to dominate classroom
groups. Among students, peer status may be based on athletic
competence or on attractiveness and popularity. Newcomers in
classrooms, especially if they are not competent in the language
of instruction, are very likely to have a low social status. Those
with a lower social standing are likely to be less active participants. In this way a group inside a schoolroom can reflect the
world of the schoolyard, even though the task is academic and
has nothing to do with play and purely social life.

Societal Status

Classrooms exhibit one other kind of status that will affect
student participation in small groups. In the society at large
there are status distinctions made on the basis of social class,
race, ethnic group, and sex. These are general social rankings
on which most people agree that it is better to be of a higher
social class, white, and male than it is to be of a lower social class,
black or brown, or female. (At least that is what people believe
in many Western societies.)

Just like academic status and peer status, societal status has
the power to affect what happens in a small group. Within interracial groups of junior high school boys who played Shoot the
Moon, the whites were more likely than blacks to be influential
and active (Cohen, 1972). This happened even though the boys
did not know each other and saw themselves as equally good
students in school. Likewise, other studies have found that men
are more often dominant than women in mixed-sex groups; and
Anglos are more often dominant than Mexican-Americans who
have an ethnically distinctive appearance (Rosenholtz & Cohen, 1985).

Why do these status differences affect participation? Why
should some students have so much influence on tasks where
they have no special competence? Why should new groups
working on new tasks reflect preexisting status orders among

the students? In order to modify this process, the teacher needs
to understand more about how and why it operates.

EXPECTATIONS AND THE SELF-FULFILLING PROPHECY

Basic to our understanding of the way in which the process
operates is the idea of a *status characteristic*. A status characteristic
is an agreed-upon social ranking where everyone feels it is better
to have a high rank than a low rank. Examples of status characteristics are race, social class, sex, reading ability, and attractiveness.

Attached to these status characteristics are general expectations for competence. High status individuals are expected to be
more competent than low status individuals across a wide range
of tasks that are viewed as important. When a teacher assigns a
task to a group of students, some of whom are higher and some
lower on any of the status characteristics described above, these
general expectations come into play. They cause a kind of self-
fulfilling prophecy to take place in which those who are higher
status come to hold a high rank in the status order that emerges
from the group interaction. Those who hold lower status come
to hold a low rank on that same status order.

From the start of the group's interaction, high status students are expected to be more competent at the new assignment; moreover, these students also expect themselves to be
more competent. This is due to the operation of general expectations for competence described above. Thus they are very
likely to start participating right away.

Low status students who are not expected to make an important contribution and who share the group's evaluation of
themselves are unlikely to say much of anything. As high status
students continue to talk, others tend to address their remarks
to them, and one of them rapidly becomes the most influential
person in the group. By the end of the interaction, this person
is likely to be viewed by group members as having made the
most important contribution to the group's performance. Thus
the status order that emerges from the group assignment is very

much like the initial differences in status with which the group started.

Returning to Shoot the Moon for a moment, when interracial groups knew nothing about each other beyond the fact that they were of different races, whites were more likely to be active and influential than African-Americans (Cohen, 1972). In this case, the group used race as a basis for forming expectations for competence in the game. Since in our culture people of color are generally expected to be less competent on intellectual tasks than whites, these racist expectations came into play in the innocent game of Shoot the Moon. Once this had happened, it was very likely that the whites would talk more and become more influential in group decision making than the African-Americans.

In accordance with Expectations States Theory (Berger, Rosenholtz, & Zelditch, 1980) the same thing happened in the Rosenholtz groups playing Shoot the Moon. Here the students used information they had about each other's standing on the academic status characteristic of reading ability to organize their expectations for competence on the new game of Shoot the Moon. Group interaction turned out to mirror initial differences in reading ability.

In the classes that Rosenholtz studied, peer status was closely related to academic status so that those students who were seen as influential in the informal social relations between classmates tended to be the same students who were seen as best in schoolwork. In other classrooms, students like Jimmy in Ms. Todd's class will have high peer status but low academic status. Students with high peer status will have the same effect on a classroom group as students with high academic status; in either case they are likely to be more active and influential than students with either low peer status (like Annie) or low academic status.

A note of caution is necessary. The operation of expectations based on status does not result in the domination by high status children of every group in the classroom. Although research finds that, on the whole, high status persons are more active and influential than low status persons, in the case of particular groups, some low status members are more influential than high status members. There are two other factors that help to account for what happens in a particular task group. These are the nature of the task, and who participates frequently at the beginning of the session.

Studies of small-group interaction almost always conclude that some of the patterns of behavior observed are a function of the peculiarities of the task that has been selected. The same holds true of classrooms. Suppose that you introduce a science task in which the group is asked to do observations of a live meal worm. Some students will be fascinated with touching and holding the worm, while others will be squeamish. Those who are fascinated are likely to be more active and influential than those who are squeamish. This ordering of behavior is linked to the peculiar nature of this task and may have nothing to do with the standing of the students on any of the status characteristics we have discussed. The nature of the task can also affect the total amount of interaction in the group. Some classroom tasks are intrinsically interesting and provoke a high level of interaction while others are boring and produce only desultory talk. Still other classroom tasks may be carried out nonverbally by manipulating the material or by communicating through writing. Such tasks will have a low level of verbal interaction, but a high level of other kinds of communication.

In addition to differences stemming from the nature of the task, studies of groups show that members who start talking right away, regardless of their status, are likely to become influential. Suppose Annie had been given the task of handing out the materials to the group. She might have had an advance look at these materials and so might have been able to explain what was to be done with them. Just such an event can change what happens in a particular group quite radically. Because the group would need to turn to her from the beginning to find out more about the materials, Annie might have become quite active in that particular group.

Recognizing a Status Problem

What are the signs of low status behavior? Low status students often don't have access to the task. They sometimes can't get their hands on materials. Body language is a good indicator of status. A student without access will frequently be physically separated from the rest of the group. Low status students don't talk as much as other students. Often when they do talk, their ideas are ignored by the rest of the group. Being treated in this way may lead to misbehavior; this is how the teacher finds out that something is amiss in the group, but scolding the low status student will do little to remedy the difficulty.

Teachers may mistakenly see low status students as passive or uninvolved. In fact, the student is simply unable to get access to the materials or the attention of the group.

EDUCATIONAL DISADVANTAGES OF DOMINANCE AND INEQUALITY

Why should a teacher be so concerned about patterns of unequal interaction in the classroom? After all, not all children have equal ability, so it is only to be expected that those who get better grades will be the most active in classroom groups. It is also only natural that those who are social leaders among the children will be looked up to, even in the classroom.

There are several good answers to this. The first has to do with learning. If you design a good groupwork task, learning emerges from the chance to talk, interact, and contribute to the group discussion. Those who do not participate because they are of low status will learn less than they might have if they had interacted more. In addition, those who are of high status will have more access to the interaction and will therefore learn more. It is a case of the "rich getting richer." In classroom research on a curriculum using learning centers, children who talked and worked together more showed higher gains on their test scores than children who talked and worked together less. Furthermore, children who had high peer and academic status did much more talking and working together than those who had lower peer and academic status (Cohen, 1984). Thus the operation of status can impair the learning of low status students during groupwork.

The second answer to the question has to do with the issue

of equity. Most teachers want to offer children equal chances to succeed in school, regardless of race, sex, or socioeconomic background. They also hope that the classroom will be a place where children who have different societal statuses will meet each other and learn that stereotypical and prejudicial beliefs held by society are not true. Teachers want children of different statuses to learn to treat each other as individuals rather than as members of particular social groups.

If status characteristics are allowed to operate unchecked, the interaction of the children will only reinforce the prejudices they entered school with. For example, if African-American children who come from poorer homes are consistently viewed in a classroom as less competent in groupwork, racist beliefs about the relative incompetence of African-Americans will only be reinforced. If the leadership position in groups always falls to boys, it will reinforce the cultural belief that "girls can't be leaders."

This reinforcement of stereotypes is not avoided by using only whole-group instruction or supervised ability groups. If the students have very little chance to interact with each other, there will be no opportunity to challenge cultural prejudices. Group interaction offers a *chance* to attack these prejudices, but the teacher must do more than simply assign groupwork tasks.

The third answer to the question of why unequal interaction should be a matter of concern has to do with the intellectual quality of group performance. In order to get the best possible group product, it is critical that each member have an equal opportunity to contribute. Listening carefully to videotapes of groups at work, I have heard some students softly and hesitantly disagree with the prevailing opinion of the group; they are on the right track and the group is not, but no one is listening to the ideas of a low status group member. If some members are hesitant to speak up even though they have much better ideas, the intellectual quality of the group's performance suffers. A second way that status interferes with the productivity of the group is through subservience to the person who talks the most. I have studied videotapes in which the group consistently turns for advice and direction to one student who, as it happens, is quite confused in her thinking, but the group persists in believing that she is the only one who has the required competence. The operation of status interferes with the quality of group performance in still another way. When two members of a group engage in a struggle over which one will be dominant, the quality of the performance almost always suffers.

From an educational perspective, what is the ideal pattern of group interaction? Over a series of groupwork assignments one would hope that different students would play influential roles depending on their ability, interest, and expertise; on the nature of the task; and on a number of chance factors. This is not to say that there is no such thing as differences in ability to contribute to tasks. When tasks are interesting, challenging and varied, each one will require different abilities, and it would seem desirable for those who are strong in these abilities or who are expert in a particular topic to do more talking and explaining and to be viewed as more competent. These inequalities become a problem, however, when a student's status on a rank order that has nothing to do with the task becomes the basis for dominance in the group. For example, we can all recognize that ability in reading is a valuable skill and that readers can make an important contribution to a group task where some students have difficulty with reading. This becomes a problem when the good reader is assumed to be better at everything and thus dominates all aspects of groupwork. When ability in one area is used as an index of general intelligence and classroom competence, you are dealing with a status problem.

This chapter has posed a dilemma: While groupwork is attractive for sound educational reasons, it can activate status problems within small groups. Chapters 4, 5, and especially 8 contain some specific suggestions about how to gain the advantages of groupwork without its drawbacks.

4 Preparing Students for Cooperation

The first step in introducing groupwork to the classroom is to prepare students for cooperative work situations. It is a great mistake to assume that children (or adults) know how to work with each other in a constructive collegial fashion. The chances are that they have not had previous successful experience in cooperative tasks working with people who are not personal friends or family members. Although many students have had some contact with cooperative learning, often they were given no preparation for that experience.

Students must be prepared for cooperation so that they know how to behave in the groupwork situation without direct supervision. It is necessary to introduce new cooperative behaviors in a training program. The goal of the training program is the construction of new *norms* or rules for how one ought to behave. Sometimes norms are written rules, and sometimes they are unspoken expectations for behavior.

When an individual comes to feel that he or she ought to behave in this new way, the norm has become *internalized*. Internalized norms produce not only the desired behavior but a willingness to enforce rules within the group. In cooperative learning settings, even very young students can be heard lecturing other members of the group on how they ought to be behaving.

Teachers have far more power than they realize in constructing new norms for classroom behavior. The beginning teacher is often told, "Be even stricter on the first day than you will actually be later on." The teacher is setting the norms for this particular classroom and is informing the students that regardless of what they may have "gotten away with" in someone else's classroom, the written and unwritten rules for this classroom are different and will be enforced.

The norms of traditional classrooms include: Do your own work; don't pay attention to what other students are doing; never give or ask for advice from a fellow student while doing an assignment in class; pay attention to what the teacher is saying and doing and not to anything else; keep your eyes toward the front of the room and be quiet. When dealing with younger students, teachers constantly reinforce these norms through repetition, reward, and punishment. By the time students are in high school, norms have become internalized to such an extent that compliant students are quite unconscious of why they behave in class the way they do.

Assigning group tasks involves a major change in traditional classroom norms. Now the student is asked to depend on other students. Now students are responsible not only for their own behavior but for group behavior and for the product of group efforts. Instead of listening to the teacher, they are asked to listen to other students. In order for the group to work smoothly, they must learn to ask for other people's opinions, to give other people a chance to talk, and to make brief, sensible contributions to the group effort. These are examples of new norms that are useful to teach before starting groupwork.

Studies of groups with no special preparation for cooperative learning suggest that if students are not taught differently, they will talk about specific procedures and will not discuss ideas or articulate their own thinking (Webb, Ender, & Lewis, 1986). If teachers want more articulate and abstract discourse, the students will need to be taught specific skills for discussion and for dealing with each other. These are not an automatic consequence of cooperative learning. Many students have no strategies for dealing with disagreement and conflict other than physical or verbal assault.

Teachers, particularly in secondary schools, feel so much pressure to cover curriculum that they do not want to take time to prepare students for cooperation. This is not a wise decision: In the long run more time is lost through disorganized group behavior than would be spent on advance training.

TRAINING FOR COOPERATION

Students need to understand your purposes in introducing
small groups and why groupwork skills are important. I was
amazed to discover that some children in the sixth grade do not
realize that adult life calls for working with people who are not
close friends. Students in one class felt that the instructors were
trying to force them to be friends with classmates assigned to
their group. When they were told that in the work world many
important tasks are accomplished in small groups of people who
are not personal friends such as research teams, fire-fighting
personnel, nursing teams, committees, and construction crews,
they were still doubtful. We then requested that they ask their
parents if this was how adults worked. When their parents con-
curred, students were willing to accept membership in groups
composed by the teacher.

Preparing students for cooperative groups requires you to
decide which norms and which skills will be needed for the
groupwork setting you have in mind. These norms and skills
are best taught through exercises and games, referred to as
"skillbuilders." People rarely learn new behaviors or convictions
about how one ought to behave through lectures or general
group discussion alone.

The remainder of this chapter will provide the principles
for your design of a training program. Appendix A contains detailed instructions for a number of skillbuilders that have
worked well for many teachers. What if none of these particular
activities exactly fits the skills and norms needed for your training program? Once you see the principles on which they are
based, you can adapt the activities described or make up some
of your own.

One note of caution about the skillbuilders: Don't judge
their suitability for your class by whether or not they seem too
easy for your students. The point of the activities is to learn how
to work together. The tasks themselves are just a vehicle for new
skills and norms, not an end in themselves. They should not be
too complex; otherwise students will be distracted from group
processes and will become too involved in the activity for its own

sake. In each case, the key to learning lies in the combination of the experience and the discussion that follows. The teacher must assist the class in reflecting on important features of what has happened and in developing key insights about the relevance of this experience to the forthcoming groupwork.

Responding to the Needs of the Group

Responsiveness to the needs of the group is a skill required of any kind of cooperative task. If students are oblivious to the problems experienced by peers, the group will not function properly, the group product will be inferior, and the interaction will not provide the necessary assistance for all its members. It is necessary that students learn how to become aware of the needs of other members of the group and to feel responsible for helping them for the sake of the group product.

One of the best ways to teach this skill is with a group exercise called Broken Circles. It was developed by anthropologists Nancy and Ted Graves (1985) from a classic exercise called the Broken Squares problem (Pfeiffer & Jones, 1970). In Broken Circles a puzzle cannot be satisfactorily solved until group members become aware of problems being experienced by others and are willing to give away their pieces of the puzzle in order to attain the group goal.

Each member of a group is given an envelope containing pieces of cardboard. The task of each group is to form circles of equal size. The task is not completed until each individual has before him or her a perfect circle of the same size as that formed by others in the group. There are specific limitations on the interaction: No speaking is allowed. Members may not ask for or take pieces from other persons. They may only give fellow members pieces that they may need. Detailed directions for this exercise and follow-up discussion suggestions appear in Appendix A, pp. 163–167.

The challenge lies in the fact that exchange of pieces must take place between members before the goal is achieved. For all but the easiest version of this exercise, some of the envelopes given to each group contain pieces that will produce a circle without exchange. However, if the person who receives such an envelope is unwilling to break up his solution and share with others, the group will not be able to solve the problem. What often happens in a group is that one of the more competitive members quickly finishes a complete shape and then impatiently waits for the others to solve their problems, gazing around the room oblivious to the struggles of other members of the group—quite unaware that he or she is the cause of the group failure.

By eliciting ideas during the postgame discussion of what made for successful or unsuccessful cooperation in the group, you can help the students gain insights about sensitivity to needs of others and sharing. Ask them how they could have cooperated more fully. This task is an excellent analog to many cooperative tasks: the individual must be concerned with giving rather than with taking or showing off individual achievement.

Do not lecture students on what they are supposed to learn from the experience. Allow them to arrive at conclusions through your questions and the discussion that follows. Then, when they have been able to develop the important insights, you can point out how cooperation in this situation relates to cooperation in the planned groupwork. Education is not magic—always make the connection between the new behaviors and the situation when you want the students to use their new awareness or skills.

Follow-up experiences

Very often it is necessary to design a follow-up experience if the groups are exhibiting problems in being responsive and sharing. An advanced version of Broken Circles (see Appendix A, pp. 166–167) allows the same class to do the exercise at a later time. Or you can provide a supplementary experience with sharing pieces of a jigsaw puzzle, as also described in Appendix A, p. 167.

Other skillbuilders that can be used to teach the same lesson include a workout with a large medicine ball where the group is given the task of keeping the huge ball in the air and bouncing for so many minutes. Here, too, the success of the group will depend on everyone's efforts. Creating a mural together can teach or review the same point about cooperation. As with the first activity, it should be followed by a discussion in which the students have a chance to draw the connections between cooperation demanded by the exercise and their own behavior in the groupwork setting.

Teaching Specific Cooperative Behaviors

Your training program should deal with specific behaviors that are required by the groupwork setting you have in mind. Start by analyzing your groupwork task. Will it be a small discussion group where everyone must come to consensus? Will it be a working group where students help each other in a collegial fashion, but are responsible for their own product, such as a completed worksheet or laboratory report? Will the task be a purely verbal one involving values and opinions or will the task involve students showing each other how things work with manipulative materials? Will the task involve creative problem solving in a situation where there are clearly better and worse answers?

Different groupwork tasks require different cooperative behaviors. To illustrate, let me contrast the behaviors called for in two groupwork settings that I have studied extensively: learning stations and small discussion groups. In the learning station format, the instructor sets up different tasks in various stations in the classroom. These might be science experiments, manipulative math problems, or map making in social studies. Tasks are typically multimedia and call for a variety of problem-solving behaviors, with more than one way to solve each part of the problem. There are clear standards by which one can judge the productions of the student as more or less successful. Students are expected to work together to help others at their station; at the same time they are expected to turn out individual worksheets or products that the teacher can examine and use as a basis for individual evaluation.

A key behavior for learning stations is helping other students. Helping others is not as simple as it sounds; the most common response is to help by doing the task for the other person. Students need encouragement in asking each other questions. They need to realize that this is a legitimate and recommended behavior at learning stations. Furthermore, they need to know how to answer each other's questions; instead of telling the "right answer," students must learn to give a full explanation. Webb (1991) found that students who received only the answer learned less than those who received an elaborated explanation.

When there is an individual product, there is a distinction between the students' finding out what others think and deciding for themselves what they are going to include in their own final report. Students need not only to be encouraged to consult with others but also to make up their own minds in creating their individual product. Finally, if students are to have a productive interchange at the learning station, they will need some practice in listening behavior. Both the questioner and the answerer must know how to listen carefully.

Although many questions concerning manipulative tasks can be answered by physical demonstration with materials, nonverbal communication is too confining as the only method of communication. Younger children need practice in *telling how* as well as in *showing how* things can be done. Younger children also need to learn new ways in which to be polite in a collegial setting; when someone gives you assistance, you should thank them or show them your appreciation in some way.

Required behaviors for small discussion groups differ in some dramatic ways from those required by learning stations. Here the task is one of verbal exchange as well as the requirement that the group reach some kind of a consensus. For example, you might ask the groups to arrive at some interpretation of literature or drama, solve a word problem in mathematics, use the assigned readings to answer a discussion question, apply what they have learned about nutrition to plan a meal, create a pantomime or role play illustrating an idea, create a five-minute conversation using new words in a foreign language class, improve the grammar and sentence structure of a composition written by a classmate, or arrive at a solution of a social or political problem.

The basic set of required behaviors includes, at minimum, the norm that everyone should contribute and that no one person should dominate the group. In addition, discussion requires

FIGURE 4.1: Student Behaviors Required in Learning Stations and in Discussion Groups

Learning Centers	*Discussion Groups*
Asking questions	Asking for others' opinions
Listening	Listening
Helping others	Reflecting on what has been
Helping students do things for	said
themselves	Being concise
Showing others how to do things	Giving reasons for ideas
Explaining by telling how and why	Allowing everyone to
Finding out what others think	contribute
Making up his/her own mind	Pulling ideas together
	Finding out if group is
	ready to make decision

listening skills. There is a tendency for members to be so concerned about saying their piece that they don't listen to what someone has just said. Not only do people have to listen to each other, but they need to learn to think about what the other person has said. Lack of listening and reflection on what others have said results in a disconnected discussion and often in a failure to reach consensus.

While older students need to learn to be concise in giving their ideas, younger students should learn to give reasons for their ideas. If the group is asked to come to consensus, then students will have to learn how to pull ideas together and to find out if the group is ready to decide what to do. Young people are typically unaware that coming to a collective decision involves some procedural discussion about how and when the group will narrow down to a decision. This is evidently learned in formal club and committee settings; even high school students do not engage in as much procedural talk as adults. A comparison of behaviors needed in the two settings is summarized in Figure 4.1.

Skills for high-level discourse

Cooperative learning can stimulate the development of higher order thinking skills. Students can hypothesize, analyze, generalize, seek patterns, and look for logical consistency in the context of a demanding task given to a group. Students often demonstrate their thoughts by stating their conclusions or by illustrating their thinking with manipulatives. They do not articulate their thinking, nor do they attempt to communicate the logic by which they reached their conclusions. In watching such groups, I can infer that the students are engaging in higher order thinking, but I would never be able to prove it on the basis of what they say. Another way of putting this observation is that students do not often engage in higher level discourse unless they are specifically stimulated and instructed to do so.

The importance of articulating one's thinking and clearly communicating ideas to others greatly increases as students move into middle school and secondary school. Unless the students can communicate scientific ideas, analysis of a social problem, or the logic behind a deduction in mathematics, they will have difficulty with advanced coursework in these subjects. Thus, despite reluctance to place so much emphasis on purely verbal intellectual production that puts some students at a disadvantage, you may decide that all students should have access to training and experience in these skills of discourse. My own experience suggests that the middle school age is the time to introduce such training. The younger students should develop their thinking skills without at the same time having the burden of translating all their thoughts into words.

Rainbow Logic is an example of a skillbuilder specifically designed to help students communicate their deductive thinking and spatial reasoning (see Appendix A, pp. 172–175). In this exercise the Grid Designer, out of sight of the group, creates a pattern of colored squares on a 3 × 3 grid, following the rule that all of the squares of the same color must be connected by at least one full side. It is the task of the group to deduce this pattern through asking a series of questions such as, "Are there blue and yellow squares in the top row?" The goal is for the players to be able to give the location of all colors on the grid after as few questions as possible. In order to achieve this goal, it is necessary for the group to *discuss and decide* before asking the gridkeeper a question. In the course of the discussion students should share the logic of their thinking. An observer is utilized to record how often players give reasons for their suggestions and whether the group really discusses suggestions before coming to a decision. In this way the students are forced to make their thinking explicit in order to share the rationale for their ideas.

As a teacher, you should think about the kind of interaction you would like to hear when you listen in on the group conversation. If it is important that the character of the group discussion be articulate and thoughtful, then you should consider using a specific skillbuilder designed to teach the kinds of "talk" you want to hear. You do not have to actually teach the words you want to hear. Rainbow Logic is a good example of an exercise that does not prescribe particular words, but encourages the students to learn to put their own thought processes into words. Any exercise that forces students to practice giving reasons for their ideas will have the same effect.

Use of social learning principles

Detailed instructions for skillbuilding exercises designed to teach behaviors such as those described above are included in Appendix A. However, if you grasp the simple principles behind the construction of these exercises, you can create training experiences for these and for any other skills you decide are important for the groupwork you have chosen.

Bandura (1969) and others have developed some relatively simple principles of social learning through extensive experimentation. These are extraordinarily useful whenever one is introducing new behaviors to children or adults. These principles may be summarized as follows:

1. New behaviors must be labeled and discussed.
2. Students must learn to recognize when new behaviors occur.
3. Students must be able to use labels and discuss behavior in an objective way.
4. Students must have a chance to practice new behaviors.
5. New behaviors should be reinforced when they occur.

Any skillbuilding exercise you develop should meet the requirements of these five principles. If you take the trouble to do so, you will have a very good chance of seeing the students make frequent and correct use of their new skills. Actually, they are learning more than the new behaviors; they are learning that these are effective ways to behave if they want a good group product. Furthermore, they are learning that these are desirable and preferable ways of behaving in groupwork situations. In sociological terms, they will be willing to enforce these new norms on their peers in the group.

Let me illustrate the use of these five principles in a skill-builder called "Master Designer" which is described in detail in Appendix A (pp. 168–170). The exercise requires a set of seven geometric shapes (illustrated in Appendix A). Each of the four persons in a group needs a complete set. The fifth member of the group is the observer. One person takes the role of Master Designer, who creates a design with the shapes. The master designer then must instruct the others as to how to replicate the design without showing it to them. Group members cannot see what the other members are doing, but they may ask questions of the master designer.

Master Designer illustrates three new behaviors. It shows students how to help other students do things for themselves. It illustrates how a group can be dependent on the master designer for explaining how a project should be done. And by virtue of another of its rules—after the master designer has certified a member's design as correct, that person may also help others by explaining how—it shows students that cooperation can lead to the group's success.

Before the exercise begins, the teacher introduces the new behaviors and assigns them labels: "Helping Students Do Things for Themselves," "Explaining by Telling How," and "Everybody Helps." These labels also appear on a poster that remains on display for the groupwork that follows training. In accordance with the social learning principles, assigning labels helps to fix the new behaviors in the students' minds; playing their parts provides them with the chance to practice the new behaviors. In subsequent rounds another student can take the role of master designer, thus giving others a chance to practice helping.

The job of the observers is to watch the group and check off every time they see two of the three new behaviors: Explain by Telling How and Everybody Helps. After each round, the observers report how many times they saw the new behaviors. According to principles of social learning, the observer role teaches students to recognize new behaviors when they occur and to discuss them with the correct labels.

It is very important to prepare the observers for their role. You cannot assume that students will automatically be able to recognize the new behaviors you have in mind—the words may have a very different meaning for them than for you. Discussing what the behaviors are and how to look for them is an essential step if everyone is to gain a needed awareness of what behaviors you are talking about. When the observers later report what happened in the groups, you have an opportunity to reinforce the new behaviors. In this way the exercise uses all five of the learning principles listed earlier.

The Four-Stage Rocket (described in Appendix A, pp. 175–176) embodies the same learning principles. A technique developed by Charlotte Epstein in her book, *Affective Subjects in the Classroom* (1972, pp. 48–57), this exercise for small-group skills has become a general favorite among practitioners of cooperative training. It can be adapted to teach a variety of needed skills for different kinds of group tasks. Other activities in the appendix are presented for the two common formats of learning stations and discussion groups. Guess My Rule (Appendix A, pp. 170–172) can be used with second graders as well as with older students, while Rainbow Logic (Appendix A, pp. 172–175) and Four-Stage Rocket (in its original form) are more suitable for seventh graders and can be used for adults as well. The exercises in Appendix A are self-explanatory.

Training during groupwork

During the course of groupwork, you will see some loss of training, some slipping back to old ways. When this happens, there are a number of strategies that you can use. The simplest is to listen in on groups; when you hear that they are not giving reasons for ideas, you ask, "Are you giving reasons for your ideas?" Or when they are not really discussing decisions before making them, you can ask: "What is the overall strategy or plan for this group? I will be back in a few minutes and you can tell me what you plan to do." You will be surprised to find that after repeating these queries for a number of sessions, you will hear the students asking these same questions of each other.

A second simple strategy is to circulate and take notes while the groups are in operation. Note good examples of use of the desired behaviors and skills as well as failures to use them and the ensuing consequences for the functioning of the group. Bring up these observations during wrap-up or before you begin the next day's session. If there have been failures of cooperation, ask the class what members of the group could have done to make the group work better.

Sometimes you will decide that serious problems in the behavior of the groups necessitate more time and attention to promoting cooperation. When this happens, take time to review important behaviors that make for a successful experience. Ask the students if they have noticed any difficulties they are having in the groups. Can they think of any way to solve these problems? Do they remember some of the new behaviors that might help? Make a public list of these behaviors. Tell the groups to repeat or extend an assignment they have already carried out. Appoint an observer for each group. The groups will work for five minutes while the observer watches for use of specific recommended behaviors. Then stop the groups and allow each group to discuss with their observer what was seen and what can be done to improve the quality of the group process. There is no need at this point to go back to exercises that are not directly related to the work at hand. The group itself has the capacity to be self-critical and to correct its problems.

During group processing, older students can work without the observer role. The entire group can undertake to become conscious of the behavior of its members. Then the group can discuss how well they are doing and how they might increase key cooperative behaviors. Research has shown that problem solving on a complex computer simulation problem was superior with a combination of the teacher giving specific feedback on cooperative behaviors and the students having a chance to reflect on how the group was behaving with respect to specific skills (Johnson & Johnson, 1990). This treatment produced bet-

ter results than either large group discussion of cooperation or
groupwork with no processing.

The secret of successful pretraining in cooperation, feedback from the teacher, or group processing is the *use of very specific behaviors*. For example, Huber and Eppler (1990) asked fifth
graders to rate their own cooperative process on general dimensions, such as friendly–hostile and hardworking–careless, and to
discuss for five minutes what went wrong during the last session
and how they could improve cooperation next time; this strategy had no effect on achievement. Apparently, this method did
not provide students with sufficiently specific information on
what was missing in their behavior and on what behaviors would
make things go better.

The behaviors must not only be specific, but they should
also be *directly relevant to the goal of the group*. This is why general
human relations training programs that emphasize sensitivity,
receptivity, openness, and reciprocity are not recommended
(Miller & Harrington, 1990). Compare these very general quali-
ties of interaction to the behaviors that the Johnsons (1990) selected for groups working on a computer simulation: summarizing ideas and information of all group members; encouraging
active oral participation of all members; and checking for
agreement among members each time a decision is made. Each
member was assigned one of three social skills and made sure
that all members used that skill.

There are additional skills, especially for group projects,
that become more important as groups attempt longer-term,
more ambitious projects. I have developed lists of helping and
troublesome behaviors for improving group process skills,
which are provided in Appendix A (pp. 176–178). Use an observer with a scoring sheet while the group repeats or extends
an assignment. The observers can report to the class as a whole
or to their own groups. This should be followed by a discussion
of whether or not the students feel these behaviors are important for achieving a better group product. The students
should also discuss alternative strategies of using helping behaviors and avoiding troublesome ones. Choose those behaviors
from the list you think will be useful for your class; don't feel
that you have to teach every single one.

Special Norms for Group Behavior

Probably the most important norm to teach when training students to discuss, to make decisions, and to do creative problem solving is the norm for equal participation. When students feel that everyone ought to have a say and receive a careful hearing, the problems of inequality and dominance discussed in the last chapter can, in part, be solved. As long as group members have internalized this new norm and have acquired some skills for discussion, students with high status are not so likely to dominate the group.

Prevention of dominance

In a laboratory study, Morris (1977) demonstrated the effectiveness of training procedures in preventing unwanted dominance in creative problem-solving groups. Here are the norms for cooperative problem-solving behavior Morris presented to his subjects:

1. Say your own ideas.
2. Listen to others; give everyone a chance to talk.
3. Ask others for their ideas.
4. Give reasons for your ideas and discuss many different ideas. (p. 63).

In order to train groups to use these norms, Morris gave them a challenging survival problem to solve. This task, adapted from survival problems developed by Jay Hall (1971), is called Shipwreck. It requires the group to imagine it is a crew of a ship sinking near a tropical island. Eight items are available to take with them from the ship. The group is asked to rank order items according to how important each is for the group's survival.

After discussing how research has shown that groups do better than individuals on creative problem solving, Morris introduced the task and instructed the group they were going to work as a team and that they would be evaluated on how well they worked together. He explained the four behaviors that make a good team effort.

To teach the group to be self-critical and to evaluate group processes, he interrupted them after they had arranged four items. He used the following discussion questions:

1. Is everyone talking?
2. Are you listening to each other?
3. Are you asking questions? What could you ask to find out someone's ideas?
4. Are you giving reasons for ideas and getting out different ideas? What could you ask if you wanted to find out someone's reason for a suggestion? (Morris, 1977, 157)

He then allowed them to finish the task and presented them with another similar survival problem. This research was able to show that the teaching of norms for equal participation prevented the high status students in these groups (those who were seen to be better at reading) from dominating the interaction.

These norms influenced behavior on a third and different task, even though it was unrelated to the survival problems and nothing was said about using these new behaviors. Students assumed that this was the best way to behave in a cooperative task. In other words, the norms had begun to influence group behavior on a new groupwork task without the adult in charge having to say anything!

Morris taught the students that if they wanted to survive in a life-threatening situation, they needed to let everyone participate and they needed to listen carefully to each other. This approach had the effect of quieting group members who tended to do too much talking and not enough listening.

How did this treatment work? Sociologically, the training introduced a new norm for equal participation along with some group process skills. Since these groups were initially unequal in reading status, we may assume that better readers thought they were going to be more competent on the survival problem. The treatment did *nothing* to interfere with the operation of these expectations for competence.

If that was the case, then why were high status students less active in the treated groups than in the untreated groups? Even though the better readers may have thought they were more competent at the survival problem, the treatment told them that they would hurt the group effort unless they let everyone talk.

Thus the new norm interfered with the process at that point where different expectations turn into different rates of talking in the group.

When treated students were asked about who had the best ideas in the group, they tended to pick the better readers. Thus we see that although the inequality in talking was reduced in the treatment group, status problems were only partially treated.

Although this treatment has only a partial effect on status problems, it is a safe, simple, and pedagogically sound way to quiet the members of your class who tend to dominate small groups. Appoint an observer in the group to monitor the use of the desired behaviors. After the reports from the observers, carry out a class discussion using the questions listed above. When you are ready to assign a groupwork task requiring creative problem solving, remind the class of the four features of group process that Morris stressed. They can be displayed permanently in the classroom on a poster.

Effective Group Functioning

When the members of a group are confronted with a challenging and uncertain task that will require a group product, they face a fundamental problem: How should they decide on the final nature of that group product, and how should they divide the labor in order to carry out the work? Suppose that a group must design a skit to dramatize the conflict between Martin Luther and Pope Leo XI. What form should that skit take? Who should write it? And who gets to play the parts of Martin Luther and the Pope? These are all questions that must be answered if the group is to have a credible product to present to their classmates.

Although it doesn't seem sensible to an outside observer, groups of middle school students will often try to move ahead without developing any general plan or strategy. Someone will say, "I think we ought to make a gold crown for the Pope." "I can cut up these pieces of paper that will look like indulgences for sale," says another person. Soon the group is busily engaged in making props, having evaded both the substantive historical questions and the issue of what form the skit will take. Given enough time, this group would eventually shape the skit, but in the middle school schedule there is not enough time to work this way. It is essential, if the group is to finish its job within time constraints, that they start by discussing the historical issues and then develop a plan or strategy.

Teachers can assist this process by creating a specific norm for effective group functioning: *Understand the issues and develop a plan or strategy for creating your group product.* This will not have much meaning for students until they have some examples. What is really useful are examples you take from listening in on their interactions. You can either report strategy sessions you overheard, or you can ask groups to share with the class how they created a plan. You can intervene when groups are floundering, and ask them to discuss the issues and come up with a plan. Be sure to return to the group to hear their plan.

A second common problem is often found in groups of middle and secondary students. When faced with making a group decision, they will take a vote rather than have a full discussion and develop a consensus. They may not even comprehend the concept of building a consensus. The drawback of voting on a plan of action is that those who are voted down then have no stake in the group product and will very likely withdraw from participation. In addition, votes often short-circuit a discussion of the intellectual issues involved. Members are too focused on the actions they will take and do not take the time to gather all opinions and examine the intellectual resources provided by group members or the materials given by the teacher.

You can introduce the norm of developing consensus in connection with the norm concerning plans and strategies. You can discuss with students what happens when instead of a full discussion, a vote is taken on what the group should do. You may want to introduce the concept of compromise. In her seventh grade classroom in Pittsburgh, California, Diane Kepner has students practice consensus-building by asking them to reach consensus on three specific items of food to have for a classroom party. After 10–15 minutes, groups report to the class their chosen items and discuss how they reached their decisions. In a second step, representatives from each group come together as a panel before the whole class to negotiate and decide on the final selection of items. The third step is critical: she discusses the group processes, such as negotiation and compromise, that were used, and the implications of these strategies for consensus-building in small groups in general.

When the groups are in operation, you can move around listening to the discussions. When you hear a group moving to a vote, you can ask, "Does everyone agree? Have you taken into consideration everyone's suggestions?" This will usually have the effect of opening up the conversation once more and emboldening those whose opinions have been ignored to make their case more strongly. Most of the time, you are not present at the critical moment when the group is taking a vote. Instead, you realize that a group is making no progress and will not complete their task successfully without your intervention. Ask them what they are attempting to do and how they reached that decision. According to Diane Kepner, they will often report having taken a vote. Then Kepner advises a teacher to say to those who lost out on the vote, "What will it take for you to feel comfortable with the group decision?" This opens the way for compromise and improved motivation to participate for all group members.

COOPERATION AND ANTI-SOCIAL BEHAVIOR

Vigorous disagreement about how to solve a problem, or about the social issues under discussion, is one of the positive features of cooperative learning and should be encouraged. Students learn as a result of being exposed to conflicting views; they are forced to justify their own views and come to the realization that there is often more than one legitimate perspective on a problem.

However, some students do not know how to handle disagreement. They may engage in personal attacks or "put downs," they may even hit each other, or they may get up and walk away from the group, feeling that their ideas have been rejected. Teachers are understandably distressed. How can students proceed with the content of the cooperative learning lesson if they have so few strategies for working together? Such behavior may be common in classes where there are many students who have had little experience with negotiation and much experience with verbal and physical violence.

Other common problems, particularly with students in the middle school, are physical and social rejection of some members of the group. They may quite directly say that they don't want a particular student in their group; or they may indicate their rejection with body language. The student may be barred from the materials with elbows and turned backs. Rejection may take the form of nonresponse to any of that person's contributions. The group may act as if he or she were invisible.

Diane Kepner is a teacher who has been trained in conflict resolution (Kreidler, 1984; Rosenberg, 1983); she applies work from this field to anti-social behavior within cooperative groups in her seventh grade classroom. Central to her interventions is the observation that conflict escalates with a cycle of blaming: "He told me my ideas stink"; "He called me a bad name"; "She told me to sit down and shut up"; and on up to "He pushed me first." If students learn to translate these blaming statements into "I feel" statements in which they express honestly how they felt in response to the other person's statement or behavior, it has a remarkable way of defusing the conflict. For example, a student might say, "When you told me that my ideas stunk, I felt like no one in this group wanted to hear anything I had to say— ever again." This provides a natural opening for the other person to explain more carefully the basis for their negative evaluation of the first person's ideas, and the path is opened to normal conversation once more.

Since this is not a "natural" way for most people to talk, it is necessary to give students the chance to practice translating blaming statements into "I feel" statements. Kepner also trains her students to follow the "I feel" statement with a positive request such as "I want you to wait until I finish before you start talking" instead of the negative statement "Stop interrupting me." Positive requests should be specific and constructive rather than vague and negative in requests for changed behavior in others. The communication worksheet Kepner uses is in Appendix A entitled Conflict Resolution Strategies for Groupwork (pp. 179–182). She has created specific examples of troublesome behavior in small groups so that students can practice "I feel" statements and positive requests.

Once students have mastered these concepts, Kepner is able to intervene in conflict situations, asking students to think about how they might replay what has happened in the group using alternative ways to express distress and disagreement. When members can talk to each other in a more constructive way, they are often able to move ahead with the groupwork. Kepner cautions that these interventions will not work if the source of the conflict is some serious difficulty between students that is of long standing, or is a product of an acute conflict that is currently taking place in the school. If students cannot put this antagonism aside in order to work together in the classroom, she changes the composition in the group, or in the case of such serious problems as gang conflicts, she may send students out for counseling with school staff.

It is not only what people say to each other that causes so much harm; it is also their body language that signals rejection, dislike, and anger. Many students are not aware that they are sending messages with their bodies. Kepner advises talking with students about what an important form of communication this is. Body language includes facial expressions, posture, and gestures. She explains that messages that are received may be misunderstood, and that a complaint of "She's giving me looks" may have no actual basis in hostility. She then divides the students into groups and tells them they are going to be given a situation to act out with only a minimum of talking. The rest of the class must then determine what the message is through the interpretation of their body language.

Kepner has selected the following situations, as examples from her experience, of what often goes wrong among students in groups:

- Two members sit beside each other and hold the book or the information card so that the other members of the groups cannot see them;

- Two group members sit across from each other and form a wedge to exclude a third member as they write and talk about their project;
- Group members actively discuss while one member withdraws;
- During a discussion group members show by facial expressions and other movements that one member's contributions are never accepted;
- As one member joins the group, another member shows that he or she wants nothing to do with this person;
- During a presentation to the class, one person shows that she or he does not want to be associated with the rest;
- During preparation for a skit, one member of the group is treated as if he or she cannot do anything right.

To follow up this exercise, Kepner observes groups in operation. Upon spotting one of these nonverbal problems, she says to the group, "Take a look at yourselves and how you are sitting and working. What are you communicating to each other?" She then leaves it to the group to figure out what is wrong and how to correct the problem.

NORMS AS A PRACTICAL CLASSROOM TOOL

Once you have completed a successful training program, the fact that new norms have been internalized is of considerable practical importance. Much of the work that teachers usually do is taken care of by the students themselves; the group makes sure that everyone understands what to do; the group helps to keep everyone on task; group members assist one another. Instead of the teacher having to control everyone's behavior, the students take charge of themselves and others.

Many educators think of training for cooperation as a kind of moral socialization; they wonder whether this is the function of schools when there are so many other objectives to be realized through public education. Although there is evidence that cooperative training will have these socializing effects, there are entirely different grounds for arguing that cooperative training is worth the time it takes from ordinary instruction. Cooperative training allows you to gain the benefits of group instruction—benefits in terms of active learning and improved achievement outcomes. If the training results in internalized norms, it has the added benefit of transferring those norms to any groupwork situation where you remind the students that the norms are relevant and useful. Most important, it frees you from the necessity of constant supervision and allows you to use your professional skills at a much higher level.

5 Planning Groupwork in Stages

Your planning process starts with a fundamental decision: How will students work together? It is this initial decision that determines the nature of the training program for cooperative skills, the second stage of planning described in Chapter 4. Cooperative training appears first only because it is the first experience of groupwork for the students.

In the third stage of planning, you create or adapt the tasks your groups will perform. In the fourth stage, you must lay the groundwork for action with great care. How are the groups to be composed? What instructions and materials must you prepare in advance? How will you physically arrange the classroom? How and when will you assign students to groups? In the fifth and final stage of planning, you decide how you will evaluate student performance.

Most of your work is completed before the students start their assignments. If your design is a successful one, you have a ready-made formula for next year's class as well as a basic format that can be repeated with different tasks for this year's class. By developing one of these designs a year, you can, before long, assemble a fine array of successful curriculum experiences as part of your repertoire.

PATTERNS FOR WORKING TOGETHER

How students work together depends on your objective for assigning groupwork and on the kind of interaction you want to hear. First, decide whether your objective is relatively routine learning or the learning of concepts, involving higher order thinking skills and/or creative problem solving. By routine objectives, I mean solving problems where there is a clear right answer or a standard set of procedures: recalling facts, understanding the assigned reading or your own lecture, reviewing for a test, applying an algorithm in mathematics, repeating a classical scientific experiment, drilling in spelling or vocabulary, or mastering map skills in social studies. Today, many teachers are using cooperative learning for such objectives.

In contrast, conceptual objectives include: learning for understanding, grasping an abstract idea in such a way that the student can recognize and work with the concept in a variety of settings, taking multiple perspectives on a problem, learning to communicate abstract ideas orally and in writing, creating a dramatic or artistic representation of a set of ideas, developing higher order thinking skills, developing an hypothesis, designing an experiment, investigating a topic in the library, and inventing or creating a solution to a problem that has no one right answer.

Second, decide on the type of interaction you want to see and hear when you listen in on groups. When groups are working on more routine tasks, you probably want to hear students asking questions and helping each other with careful and patient explanations. You want to see students showing each other how to do things or drilling each other in preparation for a quiz. In many cases, your hope is that the stronger students will be helping the weaker students so that they will receive attention when you cannot reach everyone who needs assistance.

Desired interaction in groups working on conceptual objectives does not consist of stronger students assisting weaker students. Instead, you want to hear an exchange in which people are stimulating each other with ideas and in which each person's contribution becomes input for any other member of the group. In many cases, you also hope to hear higher level discourse where members articulate their strategies, deductions, and general reasoning. There should be a playful quality to the interchange in which group members are creating physical models, pointing out patterns, and using their imaginations. They are willing to risk "far out" hypotheses and suggestions in order to stimulate the thinking of others. Participants are not overly constrained by trying to find the right answer or to say what the teacher had in mind.

Once you have decided on your objectives and the kind of interactions you want to hear and see, you already have set the stage for the way your students will work together. In the case of more routine tasks, collaborative seatwork is a common pattern: Students are given an assignment that they might ordinarily do as individual seatwork, but are told to work together and help each other. This design will work *only if* students are truly motivated to assist each other and are able to give high quality explanations. Failure to meet these conditions will leave poor achievers without the help they need to complete the task (Webb, 1991). Collaborative seatwork is an example of what I call a *limited exchange model of working together.* The major need for interaction lies in supplying information on how to proceed and information on content; and the information is likely to flow from better students to weaker students.

Turn-taking is another example of limited interaction that is suitable for routine tasks. Partners may take turns in drilling each other on spelling and vocabulary. Each group member may take turns in saying what they think is the correct answer and giving reasons. Students may even take turns playing the role of the teacher and summarizing the main points of the teacher's lesson while other students play the role of the learning listener whose job it is to ask probing questions and encourage the leader to explain better. When the measure of success is how well students retain information on a test, this kind of structured oral discussion has been found to be markedly superior to simple discussion (Yager, Johnson, & Johnson, 1985).

In the case of less routine, more conceptual objectives, the pattern of working together should be based on an *equal exchange model.* To create equal exchange you will need a true *group task* where no one person could easily do the task alone. Members will find it necessary to exchange ideas freely in order to achieve the goals set by the teacher. If one person can do the task alone, then there is no motivation for a free exchange of ideas, but the only issue is whether the person who knows how to do the job will help those who don't. To achieve equal exchange you will also want to avoid dividing the labor among participants too sharply because if everyone has their own job to do, there is no need to talk and exchange ideas. The problem given to the group for this kind of objective is typically rather uncertain, requiring the group to create a solution.

To maintain an equal exchange, you will want to encourage as much talk among the members of the group as possible. Research has shown that when there is a group task and a problem with an uncertain solution, the success of the group depends on the amount of talking and working together (Cohen, Lotan, & Leechor, 1989). Thus you want to select patterns of working together that will not constrain the amount of interaction.

In a review of research on what makes small groups productive, I came to the conclusion that improvement in measures of learning depends on matching the pattern of working together with the desired learning outcome (Cohen, 1992). For relatively lower level outcomes, the limited exchange model, with its focus on acquiring information and correct answers, is adequate and often superior. For higher order thinking skills, the interaction must be more elaborated and less constrained. Nystrand, Gamoran, and Heck (1991) make a similar distinction between groupwork tasks that are only collaborative seatwork and tasks that permit the students to define their problem and to produce knowledge on their own. On a test of understanding of literature that included conceptual questions, they found that ninth-grade classes spending more time in cooperative groups that demanded production of knowledge scored significantly higher on the test than classes spending less time in such groups. In contrast, collaborative seatwork, the most common pattern, was distinctly unhelpful in improving students' ability to deal with conceptual questions.

Individual and Group Accountability

Regardless of which pattern of working together you choose, the problem of accountability is central and must be solved. What are you going to do to make people relate to each other as if they were members of the same group? It is not enough to assign a single task to a group. Even though everyone has the same goal, some people will sit back and let others do the work—what has been called the "free rider" problem. If you try to solve this problem by giving everyone an individual assignment and telling them that they should work together and help each other, it is very likely that the group will break down into individuals doing their seatwork. Another common way to solve this problem is to give each person a part of the task, telling the group that they cannot achieve the group goal unless everyone does his or her part. Although this solution has the advantage of making sure that everyone contributes to the group goal, it has the disadvantage of providing no motivation for people to help each other and not much basis for free and unconstrained interaction.

The solution to this dilemma is the necessity for both *individual* and *group* accountability. My review of the research indicates that the best results are achieved when the design for groupwork includes both these features (Cohen, 1992). Individuals should be responsible for some kind of individual product based on their participation in the group. This individual product might be created during the time the group meets together, or it can take the form of individual performance on a test based on the academic content of the group activity, or it can be homework based on the group activity. In addition to the individual product, the group must somehow be held accountable for its collective activity. One way to do this is to require the group to turn out a product of its exchange, such as a presentation to the class, the creation of a physical model, the results of an experiment, or a group report.

Slavin (1983) advocates a different method of group accountability: competitive group rewards. After reviewing 41 studies of cooperative learning that contrasted cooperative treatments of various types with traditional, individualistic learning, he came to the following conclusion: Achievement is enhanced by cooperative learning when cooperating pupils are rewarded as a group, while each pupil is individually accountable for his or her learning. In the most widely disseminated of the various models of cooperative learning developed by Slavin and his colleagues—a technique referred to as the STAD (Student Teams–Achievement Division) procedures—individuals take a test on their own learning and receive individual grades. For the purpose of public recognition, a group score or team score is awarded that is a composite of how well each individual has done relative to his or her own past performance. Certificates of award are handed to the team with the highest score, or the winning score is published in the class newspaper, or posted on a bulletin board. Slavin's (1983) conceptualization of how cooperation leads to achievement emphasizes individual accountability as strongly as group rewards. He states: "Learning is enhanced by provision of group rewards if and only if group members are individually accountable to the group for their own learning" (p. 59).

The effectiveness of group rewards does not mean that it is impossible to hold individuals accountable or to motivate them to participate without such rewards. Group rewards are more important for the kinds of collective or collaborative seatwork tasks that I have described as examples of limited interaction, where it is necessary to motivate those who could do the task by themselves to interact and to assist those who are having difficulty. Group rewards are unnecessary for achievement when using the equal exchange model, where students are motivated to complete a challenging and interesting group task that requires everyone's contribution for a good outcome. Students care about making a strong presentation to the class. They don't want to look foolish and unprepared. Several studies have documented major conceptual achievement gains as a result of motivation by intrinsically interesting and challenging group tasks. To create individual accountability, individual reports were required or individuals were responsible for some portion of the final product (Sharan et al., 1984; Cohen, 1991).

CREATING THE TASK

Clearly the choice of task depends on what you want the students to learn. If you are teaching social studies and want the students to experience democracy in action, then you need tasks that require the group to arrive at a collective decision after proper deliberation. If, in contrast, you want the students to understand the relationship of area to perimeter, then the tasks should allow students to discover the nature of this relationship for different shapes. If the goal is more social, such as the reduction of sex stereotyping in the classroom, then you will want to select an engaging task, such as making a videotape that will allow the group to experience a highly rewarding task through cooperation.

Tasks for the limited exchange model have more in common with ordinary classroom assignments than with tasks for the equal exchange model. When objectives are conceptual rather than routine, you will want to find or create a rich multiple ability task: a task with a wider range of intellectual abilities than conventional school tasks. A multiple ability task

- Has more than one answer or more than one way to solve the problem
- Is intrinsically interesting and rewarding
- Allows different students to make different contributions
- Uses multimedia
- Involves sight, sound, and touch
- Requires a variety of skills and behaviors
- Also requires reading and writing
- Is challenging.

I will provide more information on the concept of multiple abilities in the discussion of treatments for status problems (see Chapter 8). A task does not work well for the equal exchange model if it

- Has a single right answer
- Can be done more quickly and efficiently by one person than by a group
- Is too low level
- Involves simple memorization or routine learning.

With younger students, the group task, along with a brief orientation and wrap-up, may be sufficient to accomplish your instructional objective. For example, students can learn about map coordinates by locating where each of the members of the group lives using the coordinates on a local map. With older students, the curriculum bears a much heavier load of background information and prerequisite intellectual skills, so that the group task cannot carry the major burden of instruction. Instead, the group activity is used in conjunction with textbooks, large group discussion, slide lectures, teacher demonstrations, and skillbuilding exercises.

The groupwork can be a culminating activity that allows students to synthesize and apply what they have learned in exciting ways. Alternatively, groupwork can be used to teach central concepts that are difficult to understand through reading, lecture, or discussion alone. For example, the concept of a system is both central and highly abstract in teaching life sciences. Students can discover the difference between a collection of objects and a system by taking apart and putting together a flashlight, by connecting animals and plants to form a food chain, or by creating a mechanism out of a pile of castoff objects. When older students have difficulty in reading textbooks, groupwork in an introductory phase can help the students learn to use the new vocabulary and to grasp the central concepts through manipulating objects and discussion. Then reading the textbook becomes much less difficult because one is not struggling with new vocabulary and strange concepts along with routine decoding.

If the conceptual objective is demanding, then no single group assignment will probably be sufficient for the students to gain a fundamental grasp of the idea. For many years, the staff of the Program for Complex Instruction has experienced success with the use of multiple tasks in simultaneous operation in the classroom. The tasks all reflect a central "big idea," but each task represents the concept with different materials and a different kind of product. For example, in a seventh-grade social studies unit on the Crusades developed by the Program, the central concept concerns ways in which historians learn about early historical periods. Different groups of students study castle floor plans and pictures of ruins, listen to recordings of Crusader songs, analyze the text of a speech by Pope Urban, and examine pictures of half-human infidels in the *Crusaders' Handbook*. Students spend several days on this project, so they experience each of the media: text, music, and art/architecture. Individuals write reports of their answers to the questions the group has discussed.

Each group presents products that require a variety of intellectual abilities. Students create their own version of a Crusader castle and show how it can be defended, write a song about current events that echoes the purpose of the music of the Crusades, and perform a skit illustrating how the *Crusaders' Handbook* was used to recruit naive villagers. As students present these products, the teacher stimulates a general discussion on the different sources used by historians.

PREPARING THE SITUATION

Groupwork requires careful planning in advance. An orientation session focuses the students on the major concepts underlying the activities and prepares them for the challenges of working together. Specific instructions can be written on activity cards and given to each group. Before students can begin groupwork, you must decide on the size of the groups and on who will be assigned to each particular group, as well as on the physical layout of the groups in your classroom. Unless you have thought everything through in advance, you will rapidly find yourself trying to be in six places at once, straightening out the problems your lack of planning has caused. Finally, it is necessary to plan for a wrap-up that encourages students to link their experiences in groups with your instructional objectives.

Planning an Orientation

In a general orientation session, you might decide to introduce the central concepts with a slide lecture, with a demonstration of scientific phenomena, with a movie accompanied by a discussion, or with a teacher-directed activity that serves as a warm-up. If the students need to develop considerable substantive knowledge before they can carry out the group task, it may be wise to develop a separate lesson on these materials the day before the groupwork.

The orientation can also be used to remind students of cooperative norms and roles that will be of particular importance for these activities. Do not include elaborate preparation for interpersonal and role skills in the orientation. The most common mistake is to try to place too great a burden on the orientation, often making it too lengthy, without analysis of which components can be done in advance and which components can be left to the written instructions or to student discovery. Remember that an orientation is only that; be careful not to preteach activities.

Orientations have still other purposes. If you have created a rich multiple ability task, this is the time to implement a status treatment (see Chapter 8) by discussing the multiple abilities required by the activities. Orientations can also motivate students through building connections to current events or to their personal concerns.

Written Instructions

Much of the burden of explaining what students are supposed to do can be placed on written instructions in the form of activity cards for all but the youngest children. (Written instructions work exceedingly well for second graders.) Being able to refer to written instructions, after hearing the main ideas in your orientation, allows the group to figure out what to do for themselves.

Written instructions must be clear and sufficiently detailed for the group to proceed without outside assistance. Some of the problems can be left to the group to solve. By refusing to give a quick answer to requests for help from the group and by encouraging them to solve some of the problems, you can help students learn that they have the capacity to deal with uncertainty for themselves.

The most common error in writing instructions is to provide too much detail, as if teachers were instructing an individual on how to carry out a technical task step by step. This approach, designed to provide as much certainty as possible, has a deadening effect on group discussion—there is nothing left to discuss. Also, needless confusion comes from adding too many words and alternative ways of explaining things. If you want the group to use some trial and error and to develop some solutions for themselves, tell them to develop their own ways of solving selected problems. Even the youngest groups are quite capable of rising to that challenge. You want to pose questions for students that will stimulate them to discuss, to experiment, and to discover. Don't be afraid to use big, interesting words; as long as someone in the group can read them and as long as someone knows what they mean (or can look them up), the group can function very well. My favorite example of instructions with just the right level of productive uncertainty is taken from the curriculum, *Finding Out/Descubrimiento* (De Avila & Duncan, 1980), described in some detail in Chapter 10. One of the activity cards accompanies an inflatable model of a stegosaurus, a string, and a metric ruler. It says: "Measure the waist of the dinosaur." The young students are left to imagine where the waist of the beast might be and to discover that the only way to measure is to put a string around the "waist" and hold it up to the ruler.

In working with older students who can handle more written information, curriculum units for complex instruction often have a resource card in addition to the activity card. For example, in a unit on the visual system, students are instructed to build a better eye that will have superior capacities to that of the human eye. They are to prepare a presentation to a potential developer of this eye, describing its advantages and special features. On the resource card is information about the eye of animals and humans that may prove useful. The resource card, however, does not contain the answer to questions posed on the activity card. Otherwise the resource card will remove all the productive uncertainty from the task.

Other kinds of uncertainty are unproductive for the learners. Suppose that you have not made clear that you expect the group to prepare a presentation for the class. This lack of clarity in your instructions will lead to a serious misfiring of your plans. You can avoid many of these errors by pretesting your instructions on a fellow teacher, an aide, or a parent volunteer. If the group is to make a presentation, they will need to know the time allotted, the number of members participating, and permissible or suggested forms of presentation. The answer to these questions can become standardized for your class, so that you do not have to repeat the information for every groupwork assignment.

Students must be strenuously encouraged to read the instructions and must not be allowed to plunge into the task without knowing what they are doing. This is especially likely when there are fascinating materials to observe and manipulate. Supply one or at most two sets of instructions; if there is one for everyone, students will try to read silently and there will be no discussion.

Size of Groups

Groups larger than five present problems for participation in interaction. For group discussion, I have always found that four or five is an optimal size. As the group gets larger there is more of a chance that one or more members will be left out of the interaction almost entirely.

The major argument in favor of larger groups is the need for more people for a long-term project; the larger group divides into task forces to accomplish subgoals. The challenge in this design is for the committee-of-the-whole to develop consensus on what the subtasks will be and on who will serve in the various subgroups. The teacher may have to check on the process of these large decision-making groups to ensure that everyone has had their say and has a feeling of ownership over the final decision. Remember, as the group gets larger, arranging times and places for group meetings and activities becomes more and more difficult.

A group of three has some special problems. There is a strong tendency for two persons to form a coalition, leaving the third feeling isolated and left out. For certain tasks such as drill with flash cards for spelling, a pair of students is an ideal group size. The limitation of pairs is that if the task is a challenging one requiring academic and other creative abilities, there is a strong chance that some pairs will not have adequate resources to complete the task.

Composing Groups

Groups should be mixed as to academic achievement, sex, and any other status characteristic such as race or ethnicity. This heterogeneity can be achieved by composing groups and assigning students or by allowing students to choose groups according to their interests in special topics that the groups will be studying. The mix in any single group does not have to represent the proportion of minority students or gender balance in your class. Mechanically insuring that each group has equal numbers of males and females or one or two students of color has the disadvantage of making the basis of your decision clear to the students. They will tend to focus on their fellow members as representatives of their race or gender and are much less likely to respond to them as individual persons (Miller & Harrington, 1990). As you continue to use groupwork and recompose groups, students will have the chance to work with everyone else in the class at least once, so the occasional group that is all female or all male will not do any harm. More important is the avoidance of groups that are homogeneously low achieving and thus lack resources for your assignment.

Allowing friends to choose each other for work partners is not a good idea. Students should think of groupwork in terms of work rather than play, and there is clearly a tendency for friends to play, rather than work, when assigned to the same group. Furthermore, some students who are social isolates will not be selected or will actively be rejected for group membership. Teachers sometimes feel that secondary school students will be rebellious if they are forced to work in groups that are not of their own choosing. This will not happen if you orient the class to the purpose of the groupwork and if you are firm and efficient in your assignments.

In composing groups, there are students whom you will view as problematic. A student who is far behind grade level in basic skills required for the task is one example. Students who have great difficulty in working with others should also be placed in groups with special care. These are often students who will attack, pester, and distract their fellow students to get attention, even if that attention is negative. At the younger ages, hyperactive children often represent a problem to classmates as well as to the teacher.

Place problematic individuals with at least one person who can be helpful. Particularly difficult hyperactive children should be put in a group with someone who can work with them inter-personally and prevent them from disrupting and distracting. (I often suggest a "bossy big sister" for this purpose.) A student who does not speak the language of instruction will need a bilin-gual student who can interpret. Someone who lacks academic skills will require a fellow student who is functioning at grade level; it does not have to be the best student in the class.

As the students gain practice in reading, discussing, and writing in the group setting, you will note that some problematic students develop to the point where you need no longer worry about them. The label of "problematic student" should never be seen as permanent or as indicative of unchanging characteristics of the person. Similarly, avoid seeing some students as "natural leaders." With proper training and your insistence that people play their roles, most students should be able to perform leader-ship functions.

Waste no time in letting students know their group assign-ment. Put assignments up on the board or on an overhead trans-parency, along with a map of where groups are to work. Or write the group assignment on top of individual report forms given to each student. The most efficient way to compose groups re-peatedly over the year is to make or buy a chart that has pockets for cards representing class members (available from many teacher supply houses). The labels on the rows and columns of the chart immediately inform the students which group they are in and what role they will play. The use of roles is discussed in the next chapter. Sort the cards into pockets and direct the stu-dents to check for their group assignments when they first enter the classroom. Figure 5.1 presents a sample chart.

Classroom Ecology for Groups

Discussion groups need to be seated so that everyone can see and hear everyone else, preferably in a circle. Irregular seat-ing arrangements will result in very little interaction among those who have to twist around to see each other. Station the groups as far apart as the room will permit so that they will not be disturbed by each other's discussion.

If you expect group members to work with manipulative

FIGURE 5.1: Chart Showing Group and Role Assignments

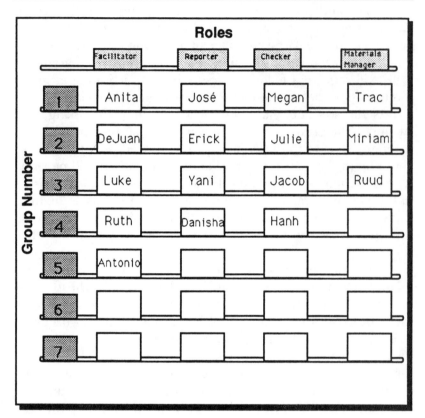

materials or with books and written materials, you must plan space for work carefully. Group members should not be kept waiting because they have no space to work. Lack of work space can result in disengagement and general failure of the projects. If members do not have adequate room to lay out their task, they may find themselves unable to solve the problems; materials tumble off the table, students jostle each other for space, and constructions don't fit together.

Work stations require rearrangements of the tables and chairs from their usual formation. Take into account traffic flow as well as the amount of workspace required. If tables are placed so that they block the free flow of traffic, students will constantly be disturbing one another. It is a good idea to map out your classroom arrangement and consider carefully how people will move about. (If your classroom furniture is inflexible and unsuitable, perhaps you can borrow the multipurpose room or the media center for groupwork.)

Noise is often a special problem for open space schools. If students are working at learning stations, a fair amount of noise is to be expected and is a sign of functioning groups. It is advisable to consult with other teachers who share an open space pod with you well in advance of scheduling groupwork. It should be scheduled simultaneously with their noisier activities.

All materials and tools should be pretested to make sure that they do what they are supposed to do. Avoid scissors that don't cut and magnets that don't magnetize. Although it may seem sensible to keep things like scissors and glue at a central location, it is actually more efficient to set these out at each learning station where they will be needed. With decentralized materials, there is far less rushing to and fro with its distracting consequences.

Teachers of elementary students must be concerned with the safety of sharp tools and with the use of heat and fire. The usual solution is to station an adult to supervise these activities directly. This is a costly solution in terms of using up scarce adult resources. As an alternative, discuss strategies for dealing with potentially dangerous materials in your orientation. Another solution is to appoint one of the children as a safety officer, with a clear understanding of what he or she should watch for and when to call for an adult.

Setting up work stations with instructions and materials sounds like too much work for the average busy teacher. It is! The students should be trained to do the work of setting up these stations; they should move the furniture and set out the materials needed. If the teacher lists or illustrates what will be needed on the activity card, the student in charge of setting up can get the materials from cupboards or storage areas, provided that these places are properly labeled (with pictures for non-readers). Another successful pattern is for teachers to prepare a plastic bucket filled with the materials and the activity cards for each center. The person in charge of materials can pick up the bucket, distribute the materials, and insure that everything is returned in proper order to the bucket after the task is completed. There is certainly no excuse for teachers having to clean up after the work is done; students will cheerfully carry out these tasks if it is made clear that this is part of their job. First graders can do an excellent job of cleaning and setting up; they appear to relish the responsibility.

Students will want to read and learn more about the subject of their group task. Especially with students who need to be encouraged to dig for information and to read books on subjects that have aroused their interest, make these informational resources easily accessible. Place relevant books from the library close by the learning station where the students are working on a particular topic. If everyone will need certain reference works, like the dictionary, put these on something with wheels so groups can easily bring the heavy volumes around to the different work stations. Display pictures, maps, costumes, and objects near the work stations to stimulate students to ask questions, think more, and dig further into the subject. A great advantage of this strategy is that if one group has finished its work before the others, the materials for obvious extension of the activity are all prepared. The teacher can, with a few minutes of discussion and questioning, help the group to push the investigation further with the materials at hand.

Planning a Wrap-Up

Wrap-up is an essential stage of groupwork. When the students make presentations based on groupwork, the whole class can share what each group has learned. When each group is doing the same task, the reports do not have to become boring and repetitive. Each group can be given a different question or aspect of the task on which to report. The teacher can weave these reports together through questions and discussion. Teachers have invented several other successful strategies. They ask the class to compare and contrast what different groups did with the same task. After each report, they use informal discussion groups to prepare questions or comments they think will be stimulating. All the reporters may convene at the front of the room as a panel of experts. Reporters are encouraged to ask groupmates for additional and/or more specific information. Above all, *vary* the way you handle wrap-up to keep it interesting.

PLANNING EVALUATION

When I present a session on groupwork techniques, teachers invariably ask: How can you evaluate student performance when the task is done by a group? To answer this question, it is necessary to disentangle the issue of learning from the issue of giving grades and marks. For most teachers, the need for students to receive feedback on their work is fused with the responsibility to give students grades.

Start with the assumption that groups and individuals need to have some way of finding out if they are "on the right track" in solving problems. They need to know how what they have done measures up to some set of intellectual criteria and what they can do to improve their product. This is the issue for learning and it needs to be considered quite apart from grading.

There are many ways to provide feedback for learning. Some groupwork tasks have the happy quality of built-in evaluation. Consider a task like making a device operate or an electric bulb light up. The students can see for themselves whether or not they are successful. If they are unsuccessful and consequently frustrated, you can help them, *not by showing them how to do it properly,* but by encouraging them to try some new strategies, to go back to the activity card, or to try out the ideas of all the members of the group. Don't be afraid to let the students struggle; this is the only way they will grasp more abstract concepts—people learn from mistakes.

It is not always necessary to evaluate whether students have grasped the ideas after each groupwork task. Some students may utterly fail to get the idea in one task but may suddenly begin to understand it in another setting. If you become overly concerned too early in the process with whether each student is mastering the content of each groupwork assignment, you will find yourself insisting that students get the right answer to every task, thus short-circuiting their whole process of inquiry.

If you want to know whether or not students are making some progress, you can and should examine the individual reports I have recommended for each group task. Students should receive specific feedback clearly stating what they did well or what could be improved. Give a reason why you think this is so. Avoid nonspecific phrases such as "very good," "great," or "fine." If you have chosen rich multiple ability tasks that have no simple right answer, then different students can learn different things from the same task. If the tasks have this open character, you will not necessarily use standardized criteria to provide feedback to individual students. Don't be afraid to inform students that they are confused about key concepts or are making dubious assumptions in solving a mathematical problem. Sometimes students will write two meager sentences when you expected a well-organized paragraph. You can ask the students to do the activity again or to rewrite the report. Even though students have received help from other group members in writing their report, they can be held accountable for what they have written.

Individuals may also receive feedback when you talk to the class as a whole:

> "I noticed that José was able to pull the whole group together by pointing out that people were not all talking about the same question."
> "When Alonso asked for help, Lila asked what she could do to help."
> "I saw today that Jeremy created a model that helped the group to figure out a way to solve their problem."

How can a group product be evaluated? You can provide feedback to the group, remembering that it should always be honest, clear, and specific about what the group did well and where it could improve. General comments such as "Great job!" may make the group feel good but they will do very little to promote learning. Do not be afraid to point out important areas of confusion in the presentations. You may not want to launch into an extensive correction of their misconceptions right then, but you can point out that there is a misunderstanding and that you expect the next group who has this group task to work out some alternative way to understand the phenomenon. If you find it difficult to listen to the presentations and to prepare your feedback simultaneously, then take notes and provide feedback on group process and products at the beginning of the next class session.

You can pick out a group that, according to its presentation, has obviously grasped the central idea or has a product illustrating an important concept, and ask members of the group to provide additional explanation of what they have learned. This has the double function of reinforcing the learners, and if you are having different groups carry out different tasks, it can prepare the rest of the class for their turn at this particular activity. Hold a discussion during a wrap-up in which group members discuss how well they have done on using cooperative behaviors featured in the training program. Remember that the class needs feedback on their group process as well as on their products.

Peer Evaluation

During any process of group interaction, there will be a constant process of peer evaluation. This is an unavoidable part of group interaction. One of the advantages of groupwork is that many students can help extend your power to teach by providing feedback to peers. Of course, you may want to include some work on giving constructive feedback as part of your training program. Peers can be merciless with each other.

If the criteria for evaluation are clear, students can learn to evaluate group products. If each group displays its work in some way, students can be taught what criteria are legitimate and how to give constructive criticism. This strategy enables the group to obtain feedback at the same time that it teaches a valuable intellectual and social lesson to the class.

Students can also evaluate how well they have done during the group process. Use the techniques of observation and self-criticism in the section on training during groupwork (Chapter 4) for constructive peer evaluation.

Testing and Grading

Many proponents of cooperative learning recommend giving a group grade for a group project. This has the effect of making individuals dependent on the group effort for a satisfactory evaluation. It has the drawback of making the peer evaluation process rather harsh. If one group member is felt to be incompetent at the task, the group is likely to forbid him or her to have any part in the product. The student who is perceived to have the most relevant knowledge will be encouraged to take over the task. It is therefore preferable to provide feedback on group products instead of grading them.

Many teachers feel that unless the group product is graded, students will not be motivated. If the task is challenging and interesting, and if students are sufficiently prepared for skills in group process, students will experience the process of groupwork itself as highly rewarding. Knowing that they will receive some feedback on their product will also help motivate them to complete the task.

Should groups compete with each other for grades or prizes on their group product? Competition has the effect of increasing motivation of students; for that reason many teachers cannot envision groupwork without external rewards. Offering competitive rewards, however, may have negative effects on the perceptions that team members have toward other teams, specifically causing them to be perceived as less personally attractive than when there is only cooperation without competition (Miller, Brewer, & Edwards, 1985; Johnson, Johnson, & Maruyama, 1984). In a socially and ethnically diverse classroom, the negative effects of between-group competition may well offset the advantages of within-group cooperation in improving intergroup relations (Cohen, 1992).

Competition will aggravate the problem of status within the group because low status students will be seen as harmful to the group's chances of winning, and it will encourage the students to believe that learning is not intrinsically rewarding but that one ought to be paid for such drudgery by something external to the learning task itself. If the tasks are rich, as has been suggested, there will be no need for such crutches to provide motivation. If the tasks are more routine, such as those found in collaborative seatwork, the mild form of competition advocated by Slavin (1983) may well be used to solve the problem of motivation. In his STAD method, the scores of students are based on the amount of improvement individuals show in comparison to the last testing; thus the team is not penalized for members whose entering achievement level is low. On the contrary, these may be the team members who will show the most dramatic individual learning gains, not only because they have received help, but also because group pressure keeps them working.

Following any series of groupwork tasks designed to teach certain skills or concepts, you can design an examination to test the individuals' grasp of those concepts. This will provide the formal occasion for grading. Use groups to prepare for the exam; students who have worked through the tasks will be well prepared to help each other.

Never grade or evaluate students on their individual contributions to the group product. Even if it were true that a student contributed almost nothing, it is never clear that the student is at fault. Other students may have acted to exclude him or her from the process. Since the individual's lack of participation may be a consequence of a status problem, it is unfair to blame the victim for the group's low expectations of him or her. Alternatively, something about the task instructions or the group process may be at fault. It is better to look on such an event as a failure of the groupwork technique rather than as a failure of the individual student. Moreover, telling students that their individual contributions will be evaluated will have the effect of making low status students unwilling to risk active participation (Awang Had, 1972).

In review, by separating the necessity for feedback in the learning process from the grading issue, the problem of what to do becomes much less difficult. Feedback can often be accomplished by peers as well as by teachers. It can take place while the groups are at work, in individual conferences with the teacher, or during a wrap-up. Including a wrap-up each day at the close of a groupwork session is invaluable for feedback on both process and product.

Teachers can meet their responsibilities for giving grades by evaluating some individual products of groupwork and by testing students for their grasp of the basic concepts the group tasks were designed to teach. Properly designed groupwork can produce major gains, even on standardized achievement tests.

A WORD ABOUT TIME

After making detailed plans, it is necessary to estimate how much time each phase will take. How much time will be needed for pretraining? Will the students have time for their first groupwork experience after the orientation? If the orientation goes on too long, the students will be frustrated by having to end the groupwork too early, or there will be no time for wrap-up. Planning groupwork for 50-minute periods in middle and secondary schools is particularly challenging. Teachers often decide to devote one period to orientation and a general warm-up activity. They devote the second period to the groupwork, along with the preparation of individual reports, and the third period to presentations and wrap-up. Making a realistic time schedule for each phase (and sticking to it) is an indispensable management tool.

6 Giving Everyone a Part to Play

Here are two illustrations of groupwork in which students play different parts. The first is a group of five fourth-grade students from an academically and ethnically heterogeneous classroom using complex instruction. The facilitator is reading the activity card with instructions on growing a salt crystal garden.

Facilitator: "What kind of changes do you see? Write what kinds of changes you see on your worksheet. If the base dries up add 2 tsp. of water and 1 tsp. of ammonia." OK? Do you understand what we are supposed to do? [The group smiles and nods. The facilitator places the activity card face down.] OK. What is the name of the center? [Group laughs. Several members raise their hand, and the facilitator recognizes one girl.]

Girl: Salt Crystal Garden?

Facilitator: You got it. [Puts card back in plastic box and directs the materials manager to hand out materials. The manager lays out the materials and hands out role badges to the facilitator, the person in charge of cleanup, and the checker who checks to see if all the worksheets are done.]

Materials Manager: Who is the reporter?

Reporter: I am. [He takes the role badge offered by the materials manager. The group spends about five minutes looking at the pictures on the activity card and working with the materials.] Hey you guys, before you begin, I have to write down the answers to this question on the reporter worksheet: What do you predict will happen in this science experiment? And don't just tell me what

you predict. I have to write down why you made this
prediction. [The group, hesitantly at first but more excitedly as they go on, begins to talk about how they
think salt crystals will form, just like in the picture.]

The second illustration is from the written report of a team
of beginning high school teachers. One of the pair worked as
the teacher and the other functioned as observer. The observer
is reporting on Mike Leonard's class in Geometry, a lower track
mathematics class.

This is a casual and friendly group of students who appear to relate well to each other and to their teacher. Mr. Leonard begins
the lecture with a short review of last night's homework. This
work covers skills needed in today's groupwork. He uses an overhead projector; the class has many questions. Mr. Leonard then
goes over the assignment. Each member has at least one equation
of a line for which he or she must find three ordered pairs in the
relation, draw the graph of the relations, find the slope of the
graph and find the y intercept of the graph. The group has the
responsibility of writing an explanation of the y = ? Mr. Leonard
has placed graph paper and a straight edge on each desk before
class.

He now reads and explains information written on the board.
This includes a list of behaviors expected in the role of facilitator:
(1) makes sure everyone participates; (2) makes sure task is completed in 20 minutes; (3) gets help from teacher if entire group
cannot answer a question.

The groups have been prearranged so that students already
know their group and their location. The facilitator's role is a ro-
tating one; and today's facilitators are given tags to indicate their
special function. One person has the role of grapher who must
graph all equations on one set of axes and label them neatly.

Next, Mr. Leonard asks the students to get into their groups
and begin work. It is apparent that he has trained his students
well beforehand because it takes less than a minute for all the students to be in groups and involved in the task. Once in their
group, certain students are still unclear as to what the task involves, but other members explain it to them. All the students certainly seem to be engaged in their work. Even those that Mr. Leonard has described as "academically weak" seem involved and
active. Some students need help in understanding how to find
ordered pairs and in graphing lines; they receive explanations

from other members of the group. The facilitators start out by leading, but as time goes by the other students are doing as much directing and "facilitating" as the person assigned to that role.

The students begin by clarifying the task among themselves and by choosing someone to play the role of the grapher; they then move into their separate tasks, working out their lines and points. The graphers are interested in pushing everyone to complete and pass the graphs on to them so that they can finish their job. In the last phase, the collective group discusses an explanation, while the graphers produce their summary graph. The assignment is done in twenty minutes. Mr. Leonard now puts up on the board the graphs from the groups—all are correct. He writes the equations on the board and proceeds to ask questions. Interestingly, several groups are able to give variations on the correct answers. This takes ten minutes, and there are still five minutes left to hand out a review sheet for the test tomorrow and an evaluation questionnaire on the groupwork. (Kinney & Leonard, 1984, pp. 9–12).

EFFICIENT AND EFFECTIVE GROUPS

How do the groups in these two illustrations avoid problems of nonparticipation and interpersonal difficulty? The secret of their success lies partly in their teachers' careful planning and preparation and partly in the way members have something specific to do. When each person's job is given a name and is accompanied by a list of expected behaviors, group members have been "assigned specific roles to play." Members feel very satisfied with their part in the group process in groups with different roles and/or jobs to do; such groups can work efficiently, smoothly, and productively. The use of roles alleviates problems of nonparticipation or domination by one member.

In the case of complex instruction, notice that the roles students play, such as facilitator and reporter, are not parts of the task that the activity card describes. Instead, these roles relate to *how the work is to be done.* For example, the facilitator is checking for understanding of the activity card and the reporter is stimulating scientific thinking and discussion about the task. I refer to these as the "how" roles. In addition to playing a "how" role, everyone must function in the discussion of the task, in the creation of the group product, and in filling out an individual report. Through the assignment of "how" roles, the teacher delegates to group members many of the tasks that the teacher ordinarily does: keeping the group on task, insuring good social relations, organizing and clean-up, and summarizing what has been learned for the class as a whole.

When each group member is doing a part of the job, there is a *division of labor*. Mr. Leonard's assignment is an excellent example: each student has to do one equation, but the results of all equations are necessary to the final product. When a specialized part of the assigned task has a name and specific expectations for behavior, I call it a "what" role. "What" roles refer to the substance of the group's assignment as opposed to how the group goes about its business. The grapher is an example of a "what" role; in order to complete the task the grapher has to take everyone's equation and graph it into one final product. Notice that Mr. Leonard combines this with the "how" role of a facilitator who makes sure that everyone participates, sees to it that the job gets done on time, and seeks the teacher's help if necessary.

"HOW" ROLES

The roles used in complex instruction helped to insure a high-quality discussion and a group product that was on track and on time. By having a materials manager, only one person needed to move about the classroom gathering construction materials for the group. The clean-up person directed the group in wiping down the table so that the teachers did not have to pick up after the children. The facilitator helped those students who could not read the instruction card and saw to it that people carried out their roles. Finally, the reporter, by requiring the whole group to discuss what he would report to the class, ensured a thoughtful presentation based on a thorough exchange of ideas.

Leadership Roles

There are advantages to the use of leaders. In the adult world of work, there are very few leaderless groups. When one person is an appointed leader, there is less jockeying for influence among the members than in leaderless groups because the status order is clear (the leader is in charge); the leader is seen as legitimate, that is, backed up by higher authority. When every decision does not have to be made by consensus, the group's operation is quicker and more efficient.

The teacher has it well within his or her power to appoint group leaders for each of the collective task groups. Furthermore, the teacher has the authority to say exactly what the group leader has the right and duty to do with respect to the group.

From an educational point of view, the use of a strong leader has some drawbacks. Group members may have very little to do with each other and may simply respond to the leader's directions. If the task involves a group discussion, a strong leader is likely to dominate. Members will tend to listen more to the group leader concerning the content of the task, even though other group members may have more valuable ideas. Furthermore, if the leader is constantly saying whose turn it is to talk, the amount of interchange between group members is greatly reduced. A leader with the power to direct discussion and to make final decisions will often cause the group to give up and to let the leader do the whole task.

Limited Leadership Techniques

How can a teacher gain the efficiency of a leader without sacrificing the active learning that takes place during creative interchange? If the leadership role is properly structured, one can have the benefits of creative interchange and the efficiency of a leadership role for a short- or long-term task.

A facilitator who acts as a limited leader is not a boss with executive decision-making rights. Everyone in the group understands that the facilitator does not have control over the decision or the content of the discussion. Instead, the role is limited to functions such as seeing to it that everyone participates, keeping the group on task and away from irrelevancies, and/or making sure that the group makes clear decisions in the time the teacher has allotted. Facilitator roles can be tailor-made for particular tasks and classes.

The use of such a limited leadership role has the advantage of efficiency because one member is in charge of the group process. It has the added advantage of preventing status struggles and domination by members of the group who have high academic or social standing. No doubt something in the way of a free and full exchange of the well-trained leaderless group is given up, but like so many decisions in designing groupwork, there is a tradeoff in the relative advantages and disadvantages of each strategy.

Research on complex instruction has demonstrated that the use of facilitators boosts the rate of talking and working together in the group (Zack, 1988). When the facilitator asks if everyone understands the activity card, the group often engages in a good discussion of what they are supposed to do and what strategies they will employ. Also, conversations will take place as help is delivered so that people are not left on their own to struggle with the task.

Group Harmonizer

A group harmonizer can ease interpersonal conflicts that arise, can be attentive to the feelings of individual members, and can encourage members to compromise and discipline themselves to help maintain the group. You can adapt the harmonizer role differently for different age groups. The youngest students may only be able to comment favorably on other's ideas. The version of the harmonizer role that we use in the middle school includes the following responsibilities: Make sure communication lines are open; do not allow "put downs"; encourage positive responses.

Roles for Older and Younger Students

With more mature groups who have the task of synthesizing individual productions into a written or oral report, an excellent specialized role is that of summarizer (or synthesizer). The summarizer works with a chalkboard or butcher paper in front of the group, noting key ideas under discussion. The summarizer is not merely recording; he or she leaves out irrelevant issues and highlights disagreements between ideas that will need to be resolved. The advantage of this role is that it tends to depersonalize disagreement; the argument is between *ideas* rather than between individuals who proposed the ideas. The group gains objectivity, and those who are unwilling to say negative things about each other's ideas face-to-face are able to be objectively critical when faced with ideas-separate-from-persons.

Another useful role for older students is that of resource person, who is responsible for helping the group to use the materials relevant for discussion. I often plan a lesson around a mini-lecture accompanied by a handout concerning the major concepts. In the groupwork task that follows the lecture, the groups are asked a series of questions that requires them to use and to apply the concepts. The resource person uses the handout, often searching out answers to questions raised by the group during the discussion. In this group design I also employ a facilitator, a spokesperson, and a synthesizer. In other designs, the resource person can look up relevant information in reference works and/or the textbook.

A recorder can provide the group with notes or a diagram from the discussion. This is particularly useful in helping individuals finish their reports as well as in creating the group report. The recorder can also make sure that everyone completes an individual report.

The reporter is a frequently used role for younger and older groups of cooperative learners, but rarely achieves its full potential. Unless the role is properly developed, the reporter struggles, in the final minutes of group activity, to think of what to say. The resulting product may be so scanty that the class has no clear idea about what this group discovered. Or the report may bear little resemblance to the actual conversation of the group. Teachers often complain that reports are boring and repetitive and that the class is restless and inattentive.

For a successful report, it is necessary that the reporter hold a discussion with the group about what is to be said. The group may decide that several people should participate in the report. The reporter who lacks self-confidence or proficiency in English may request that other group members accompany him or her to the front of the room to assist. If the group product is a role play or the presentation of a concrete construction, the reporter may act as announcer or narrator, briefly summarizing the activity to introduce the presentation to the class.

In a study of the reporter role, Ehrlich (1991) experimented with stopping the group for a formal discussion similar to that held by the reporter in the first illustration in this chapter. The reporters were given a special worksheet and time to discuss with the group the answers to a set of questions in preparation for their report to the class. The enhanced reporter's job was to encourage the group to think and talk together, and as a group, to answer questions on the special form. These questions were timed at the beginning of the task, in the middle, and at the end. They were designed to encourage science-thinking behaviors. For example, the group was asked to specify their predictions for the science experiment, their observations, the inferences from their observations, and the extent to which their predictions were supported by their observations. Fourth-grade classes receiving this treatment were compared with classes using the same curriculum and techniques for cooperative learning, but with no special preparation or worksheet for the reporter role. Classroom observations revealed that students interacted more frequently when they used the reporter form than when it was absent. On a criterion problem-solving task at the end of the year, groups from classes that had experienced the enhanced reporter role demonstrated more science-thinking behaviors. These behaviors included asking thinking questions, requesting justification, predicting, hypothesizing, inferring, and concluding. Ehrlich felt that fourth graders were the youngest students who could manage these challenging discussion questions.

Young children love to play roles that entail clear responsibilities. Children preparing a salt crystal garden at the start of this chapter illustrate the set of roles used by teachers of second through fifth grades for *Finding Out/Descumbrimiento*, a bilingual curriculum designed by De Avila and Duncan (1980), to develop thinking skills. The system of classroom management I created for this approach was the initial version of complex instruction: heterogeneous groups of four or five children assigned to each of five or six learning centers. All classrooms use facilitators;

teachers select from the other roles on the list below to suit their own situations:

Facilitator: Sees to it that everyone gets the help he or she needs to do the task; is responsible for seeking answers to questions within the group; teacher is only queried if no one in the group can help.

Checker: Makes sure that everyone has finished his or her worksheet, answering all the questions.

Set-Up: Is responsible for setting up all the materials at the learning center. These are stored in such a way that a child can easily gain access to the materials needed. Pictures help to tell the child which materials will be needed and where they will be placed.

Clean-up: Is responsible for putting away materials properly and wiping off the table.

Safety Officer: Is responsible during tasks involving heat or sharp edges for supervising others and for notifying adult of potentially dangerous situations.

Reporter: Is responsible for telling what the group found out during the wrap-up.

DIVIDING THE LABOR

There are so many ways to divide up the work within groups and between groups that the actual limit is set only by the teacher's imagination. To provide an idea of the possibilities, let me present three examples.

Constructive controversy, developed and evaluated by the Johnsons (Smith, Johnson, & Johnson, 1981; Johnson & Johnson, 1985), illustrates a method in which an elaborate use of "what" roles and shifting division of labor successfully foster higher level discussion leading to conceptual understanding. In one study of constructive controversy, students worked in four-person groups over several classroom sessions. First, two-person pairs, having been provided with relevant information, prepared opposing sides of a debate concerning conservation vs.

economic interests on the proposed reintroduction of wolves into Minnesota. Within the pairs each student played a relevant role, such as farmer or rancher. Second, the pairs presented their opposing sides. The opposite pair was motivated to listen very carefully because the third phase required the pairs to switch sides and argue, using the information that had been presented. In the final phase, the entire group had to arrive at a consensual view of the issue and to write a group report. In quality of discussion and on a test of understanding, this method was found to be superior to either conventional debate or simple discussion groups.

A second possibility is the expert technique: Divide the class into groups with each group asked to prepare the answers to a different set of study questions. Students are told that they must make sure that each person in the group will be able to function as an expert on the answers to their set of questions in the second phase. For the second phase, divide up the experts so that there is one expert for each set of questions in each group. Then instruct the group to go over all questions, with the resident expert acting as discussion leader for his or her set of questions. This is an adaptation of Aaronson's Jigsaw Method (1978). I would recommend it only for classes where students are fairly secure in reading skills. Otherwise, an "expert" may experience public failure because he or she cannot really master the study materials.

As a third possibility, break up the task so that each person plays a different and complementary role; a technical group such as an airplane crew or an operating room team operates in this way. People work together very closely, but each has a different job to do—all examples of "what" roles. I used this method with success at the Center for Interracial Cooperation, a summer school where students made movies in interracial groups (Cohen, Lockheed, & Lohman, 1976). The roles were divided into camera person, director, story writer, actor, and so forth. Over the weeks of the summer school, each student played every role. For the interracial situation this technique had the great advantage of teaching the students that if given the chance to play a specialized role, different people can make very different and creative contributions to the group.

Dividing the labor and the use of "what" roles have two special problems. The first is that of getting help for the persons who cannot play their specialized role unaided. Many teachers try to solve this problem by selecting those students who have already shown special talents for particular roles such as story writer or actor. However, this strategy has the unfortunate effect of pigeonholing people and not allowing them to expand their repertoire through trying new roles. The second problem is that of maintaining group interaction and an exchange of ideas. If everyone is doing their job, there may be no basis for interaction.

The technique of constructive controversy uses roles such as rancher and farmer, but each side of the controversy works in complementary pairs to use written materials and to build a case. Thus, a poor reader could receive assistance. Secondly, the group has a final integrating phase in which everyone collaborates equally to propose a final report, thus solving the problem of insuring interaction.

In the second example, the expert group provides assistance to any member who is not confident of playing the expert role for the second phase. The group rehearses some of its members if necessary. Thus no one who is supposed to be "expert" is left to flounder. Although students play specialized roles as experts on particular questions in the second phase, they work together as a leaderless group in the first place, thus insuring exchange of ideas.

In the third example of the movie crew, the task is one in which the roles work very interdependently. They must interact extensively while they work and while they view the results of their attempts at filming. Moreover, the roles rotate so that no one is pigeonholed as an actor or as a camera person.

ASSIGNING ROLES

How can you make sure that students will accept roles that you assign and will be willing to play them? There are three things you must do to insure the effectiveness of any assignment of roles:

1. Make your assignment of the job to a specific member of each group public knowledge—everyone must clearly know that you have given this person the authority to act as facilitator or reporter.
2. Specify exactly what the person playing the role is supposed to do.
3. Make sure that everyone knows what the role player is supposed to do.

Try writing out the prescribed behaviors for each role on a large card and post them on the walls. This will help to clarify the role; it will also make everyone understand that the facilitator (or any other role player) is only doing what the teacher has directed. When this is done, even the meekest student will be willing to step forward and be a facilitator if you ask, and group members will treat that person with respect.

Strong, clear assignment of roles is particularly important for leadership roles. Suppose the facilitator tries to quiet down someone who is doing too much of the talking: "I think the group understands what you've been saying; we need to hear some other ideas." Unless the target of this remark understands that the job of facilitator involves giving everyone a chance to contribute, he or she is likely to view such a remark as a personal insult. The object of all this clarity, specificity, and publicity is to have group members understand that the leader is behaving in a certain way only because he or she is expected to do so as part of the job.

In selecting students for leadership positions, don't try to pick people on the basis of "leadership quality." Give everyone a chance to play the role of facilitator at one time or another. Because teachers often believe that few students have the capacity for leadership roles, they tend to pick the most successful student or the most popular or athletic student. Natural social leaders are also picked for a very practical reason: Teachers are sometimes afraid that unless they win over such students, they will be a source of trouble during the groupwork.

It is true that under ordinary classroom and playground conditions only a few students are capable of persuading others to do as they say. But the conditions in groupwork are different in important ways. The facilitator does not have to assert leadership in an informal group. Instead, he or she has been *assigned* to play a specific role in a specific group by the teacher. Under these conditions a student with ordinarily low or middling status in the classroom will have little difficulty in guiding a group. If the role is clearly and publicly defined, and if students are properly prepared for any skills that will be called for (see below), a wide variety of students can be excellent facilitators.

The opportunity to play such a role is a much-needed boost to the status of many students in the classroom who are seen as meek, mild, or incompetent. It is especially important that girls get the chance to play leadership roles; very few girls are spontaneously seen as leaders by teachers or by peers (Lockheed, Harris, & Nemceff, 1983). When girls were given the chance to play the role of facilitator in cooperative learning, Leal (1985) found that girls were just as likely to be seen as leaders as boys. When there are only a few minority students, appointing one of them to play a leadership role is important in combating the sense of powerlessness they may feel in a classroom with few students like themselves and in a school with few teachers or administrators of their racial or ethnic background.

When a low status student attempts to play the role of a facilitator, you will sometimes see group members literally take the role away and play it themselves. Watch out for this occurrence, and be careful not to let it happen. Hold students accountable for playing their own roles. It is easier to do this when everyone is wearing a badge indicating their particular job in the group. Then you and everyone else knows who is supposed to be doing what.

If you let the group choose their own roles, they will tend to give whatever they perceive as the most desirable and powerful role to the student with the highest status. Since you don't want to reinforce the status order that already exists in your classroom, this is obviously not a good idea. Make it clear that everyone gets a chance to play every role through systematic rotation of jobs. The easiest way to do this is through the use of a chart (described in the last chapter) where the labels of rows represent the various roles. Students can see that you are systematically moving their name card down the chart with each new group assignment, so that they play new roles each time, although the other members of the group may vary.

DEVELOPING ROLES

Roles have become very popular with teachers who use cooperative learning. However, on my classroom visits and when I observe groups in my own classes at the university, I often find that people are not playing the assigned roles. Why does this happen? Teachers often fail to check, as they move around the room, on whether or not roles are being played. Also, students don't feel comfortable and able to behave in the new and different ways specified for their position. Roles take much more development and learning than teachers imagine.

The younger the student, the more time it takes to develop clarity and skills for these roles. Younger children have had much less experience in playing a variety of roles than older students and adults. Playing these roles is related to drama; therefore it helps if students have some standard phrases to get started. For example, a facilitator can say, "Does everyone understand the activity card?" A harmonizer can ask if everyone feels OK about the decision the group has reached. In an initial discussion of roles, the class can develop some scripts under your direction. Students need a chance to practice these new behaviors, so you can have students pretend they are in groups and practice their roles.

Furthermore, these roles must be discussed and reinforced in the wrap-up following each session. Observe how people are playing their roles and take notes as you move around the room. Raise issues for class discussion based on your notes; bring out good examples and examples illustrating the need to develop some alternative strategies. Write the new strategies down and provide practice opportunities. And do not be afraid to point it out if people are not playing their roles and to ask the group to take care of this problem.

Training Facilitators

Suppose that you want a facilitator to ensure a rich discussion. Typical fifth graders do not have a clear idea of what a good discussion is, nor do they have many tactful strategies for persuading group members to change their behaviors. There-fore, unless you are sure they have the skills, it is wise to train the potential facilitators to carry out their jobs.

Wilcox (1972) demonstrated that it is possible to train fifth- and seventh-grade students from inner-city classrooms to be successful facilitators. In her study, students in groups with trained student leaders were significantly more active than students in groups with untrained student leaders. The results with untrained student leaders were highly variable; some looked as good as groups with trained student leaders while the techniques of others left much to be desired.

She chose student leaders who were neither the most nor the least socially powerful members of their classrooms. Those students selected as trained student leaders were given the job of helping the group in meeting the three criteria for a good group discussion: Give everyone a fair turn; Give reasons for ideas; Give different ideas. During the initial training session groups leaders were told the following:

> "There are different ways a person can be a leader. Different people have different ideas about what it means to be a good leader. Some people think being a leader means telling everyone what to do practically all the time. Some people think a good leader means letting everyone do just as he pleases—not interfere with their fun. And some think—and this is my idea too—that a good leader is in between these two. I think being a good leader means being part of a good group—talking with the other members—letting everyone tell his ideas—being just like the other members—so long as everything is going okay.
>
> But if things are not okay, then the good leader knows how to help his group. When wouldn't things be going okay? (Children may suggest, and if not, trainer mentions the silent group, the non-participator, the monopolizer.) If someone in the group never gives anyone else a chance to talk—or if one person doesn't talk—a good leader can help by asking questions—or reminding the big talker that someone else needs a chance. We'll talk about how to do this without making others angry. But remember—the good leader uses these ideas only when they're needed. Most of the time the good leader is just like everyone else in the group listening and taking turns talking." (Wilcox, 1972, p. 145)

Wilcox rehearsed with the leaders how they could get the group to adhere to the criteria. The students then role-played a discussion such as they would lead. They were directed to stop the group discussion after about five minutes and ask members to evaluate how well they were doing by the criteria on the suggestions chart.

Note the way Wilcox stressed a limited leadership role, so that the student leaders would not become dominant, particularly in the area of the final group decision. She made sure they would recognize undesirable leader behavior by making a special training film, but there are less elaborate ways to accomplish this objective. One might role-play the leader who dominates the group discussion, or ask one of the students to play this role, or one might tape record a simulated session with an overly dominant facilitator.

This is not the only way to train facilitators. However, it does illustrate the importance of clearly defining the role and carefully preparing new skills. Regardless of the age of the students, the instructor should always try to achieve this kind of clarity and should stop to analyze whether or not appointed facilitators have the skills necessary to carry out the role.

LONG-TERM PROJECTS

For long-term projects, it is possible to use leaderless groups for selected phases. Keep in mind that consensus groups with no formal leadership and no division of labor are very costly in terms of interpersonal relations and the level of social skills required. They are likely to exhibit status problems where one person dominates the group or status struggles in which several persons grapple for dominance. Therefore, only short-term use of such leaderless groups is recommended.

If the project is long-term, one possibility is to pull out those stages or phases of the task in which exchange and creative problem solving are most critical. These particular stages can have a leaderless group structure, while all the rest of the project can benefit from combinations of division of labor and special roles for different group members, including leadership roles.

Recall that creative interchange will not be accomplished without some sort of special training and socialization of norms for behavior during group discussion.

Two of the stages of a long-term project that benefit from creative interchange are the initial planning session and the integration of the final product. Obviously the project's outcome is largely determined by the depth of the analysis of the problem and the quality of decisions. If the students are discussing a social studies project on Pueblo dwellings, their final report or presentation is only as good as their analysis of which important materials are to be gathered and which activities are to be carried out by individual group members. At a more advanced level of scholarship, if the group is asked to do some library research on one aspect of a particular theme in order to write a group paper, the quality of that paper is dependent on the initial intellectual analysis.

In addition to this primarily intellectual reason for desiring a thorough and open discussion of the initial plans for the project, there is an important social–psychological reason for making everyone an equal and full participant in the initial planning phase. Unless members feel that they have a strong stake in the decisions made, they are likely to lose motivation when difficulties develop in carrying out their tasks. If, in contrast, all feel that they have had a fair chance to contribute to initial plans and have accepted the group's decision after arguing the issue fully and accepting or compromising in some reasonable fashion, there will be fewer if any members who let the group down by failing to do their jobs. Other members will feel free to say, "You took part, and you agreed that this was a reasonable way to do the job. So now you have to do your part!"

When the pieces of the final product have been assembled, the group is ready for another phase that requires an open interchange. A leaderless group can be used once again at this time. Particularly if the group has been through a period where members have been on their own, researching or creating materials for the final product, the group needs to learn what each member has found out. Although some of this process can take place through reading and examining the production of individual members, major intellectual benefits come from evaluating, analyzing, and synthesizing what each person has learned. This discussion can cause the group to look at the problem in new and different ways. Integration is a challenging task intellectually as well as interpersonally. Criticism and evaluation from others are never easy to take, but they are essential for a good final product.

During the middle phase, when the labor has been divided, people can go about their business in a fairly independent way. At this stage, it is desirable to have a leader who acts as a center for group communication and who keeps everything moving forward.

Group Investigation

Group investigation, developed by Sharan and Hertz-Lazarowitz (1980), is the most sophisticated method for long-term projects using planning groups, division of labor, and "how" roles for group management. Repeated evaluations in heterogeneous classrooms have shown that it is particularly effective in teaching concepts requiring higher level cognitive skills and in producing more cooperative and altruistic behavior (Sharan, Hertz-Lazarowitz, & Ackerman, 1980; Sharan & Shachar, 1988). More recently, Yael and Shlomo Sharan (1992) have prepared a book on this method for teachers.

In group investigation, students act as creative research scholars, producing their own knowledge. In order to achieve these goals, they must work together closely. Good group process is insured in various ways: building commitment to the group and its project, use of division of labor, and group process skills. If your objective is to enable students to create their own knowledge, and if you have been successful on short-term tasks with skills for group process and with the use of "how" roles and the division of labor, you may wish to plan such a long-term project. Be forewarned that group investigation demands the combination of all these strategies as well as skillful support and supervision by the teacher.

7 The Teacher's Role: Letting Go and Teaming Up

Question: What is your most important insight about teaching that you wish you had known during your first two years of teaching?

Answer: To let kids do more and me do less. This has been a hard lesson to learn over the years. I use a lot of cooperative learning, hands-on activities, and inquiry in the class and it was difficult for me to learn to step back and let it all happen. (Paul Martini, Woodside High School science teacher, Woodside, California)

Groupwork changes a teacher's role dramatically. No longer are you a direct supervisor of students, responsible for insuring that they do their work exactly as you direct. No longer is it your responsibility to watch for every mistake and correct it on the spot. Instead, authority is delegated to students and to groups of students. They are in charge of insuring that the job gets done, and that classmates get the help they need. They are empowered to make mistakes, to find out what went wrong, and what might be done about it.

This does not mean that you have given up your position as an authority in the classroom. On the contrary, you are the authority who gives directions for the task; you set the rules; you train the students to use norms for cooperation; you assign students to groups; you delegate authority to those students who are to play special roles; and, most important, you hold the groups accountable for the product of their work. This chapter discusses what letting go while groups are operating means for your role.

Groupwork is better done with the aid of a colleague or some other adult. Designing and evaluating groupwork tasks is a classic case of creative problem solving where "two heads are better than one." Considering that teachers have responsibility for their own classrooms and are not free, let alone welcome, in other teachers' classrooms, you may feel that this is an impractical recommendation. Solving this problem is the second topic of this chapter.

DELEGATING AUTHORITY

When you stand in front of the class and instruct the students as a whole, when you give out individual seatwork and walk around the classroom overseeing performance, when you divide up the class into reading groups and sit with one group while they take turns reading aloud or answering your questions, you are using direct supervision. Even when in preparation for groupwork you gather the class together and provide an orientation, you are using direct supervision.

When groupwork is underway, however, and groups are working and talking together using the instructions you have prepared, then your authority has been delegated. The teacher cannot possibly be everywhere at once trying to help six different groups. Moreover, having students talk with each other is essential as a method of managing heterogeneous classes. When they are trained to help each other, perhaps by reading or by translating into the student's native language, students use each other as resources to understand the assignments.

When students are working on uncertain conceptual tasks such as discovery and creative problem solving, talking and working together are a necessity for achievement (Cohen, Lotan, & Leechor, 1989). Students must be encouraged to work with each other to deal with all the questions and problems involved in these tasks. Research has shown that all students, but particularly individuals who are reading below grade level, benefit from interacting with other students on challenging tasks

(Leechor, 1988). Unless you are successful in delegating authority to groups, your students will not gain these benefits of talking and working together and you will find that groupwork is unmanageable.

An Effective Management System

Teachers are always surprised to discover how smoothly students can operate on their own in properly designed groupwork. The secret of successful management of such complex instruction lies in clarity—the students' perfect understanding of how they are supposed to behave, what they are supposed to be doing, and where they can turn for help if problems develop. The same is true for a traditional classroom; the difference is simply that with groupwork, students have to take more responsibility for their own behavior and for the behavior of others in their group. They should not be turning to the teacher for constant direction, evaluation, and assistance; they should use their peers instead.

Clarity is attained by having as simple a system as possible. In addition, much clarity is achieved by training in advance for roles and for cooperation, as well as by the careful planning process recommended in the preceding chapters. All these management techniques operate to control student behavior in a constructive and productive manner without having to tell people what to do directly. There is no need to control individual students' behavior with systems of points or rewards; the teacher's job is to make the groups and the instructions operate to solve any discipline problems that arise.

The steps for developing such a management system are briefly summarized below:

1. Cooperative norms need to be taught as recommended in Chapter 4 so that students will know how they ought to behave and will act to enforce these behaviors on others.
2. Students should know which group they are in and where that group is supposed to meet; a minimum amount of time should be wasted in getting across this vital information.

3. Public and specific information as to who is to play what role and what specific behaviors are expected should be available as described in the previous chapter.
4. Each group should have clear instructions for the task available to them as they work; this will do much to prevent students from having to turn to you as a source of knowledge.
5. Students should have heard a brief orientation from you on the objectives of this task and on the criteria for evaluation.

For many groupwork situations, these five considerations will be quite sufficient for everything to go smoothly. You may also want to select a set of fundamental rules and keep these posted. In the implementation manual for complex instruction in the middle school (Cohen & Chatfield, 1991), we recommend the use of the following basic rules:

- You MUST COMPLETE each group activity and individual report.
- Play your role in the group.
- You have the right to ask anyone else in your group for help.
- You have the duty to assist anyone who asks for help.
- Help other group members without doing their work for them.
- EVERYBODY HELPS.

When you use collaborative seatwork, the written worksheet or assignment directs the students as to what you want them to do. When the task is more conceptual and involves discovery, I recommend the use of an activity card. Many of the published curricula featuring cooperative learning in science suffer from an inadequate delegation of authority because of the lack of an activity card. The students rely on directions from the teacher, who frequently interrupts the group to give directions and to assist in the process of discovery. The teacher is concerned that the students get the "point" of the activity and tries to prevent the group from making errors while discovering what they are supposed to be discovering. The difficulty with this procedure is that it greatly reduces the amount of talking and working together. The group has no chance to achieve its own insights and individuals who are lost are unable to use other group members as resources.

The "No Hovering" Rule

Following an orientation, you delegate authority to groups to carry out their task. It is of critical importance to let them make decisions *on their own*. They even need to make some mistakes on their own. They are accountable to you for their work. You must let go and allow the groups to work things through without your overseeing every step. They must learn to solve some problems for themselves.

Teachers in traditional classrooms, when they are not lecturing, spend the bulk of their time guiding the students through various tasks. They show and tell how to do the assignments. They redirect students who appear to be disengaged from their work. They answer many questions that come from individual students.

This kind of direct supervision will undermine the management system you have worked so hard to develop. If you are available to solve all the problems, students will not rely on themselves or on their group. Because of their past experiences with supervision, whenever students see you hovering nearby, they will stop talking to each other and look to you for direction. If the teacher attempts direct instruction while the students are engaged in the groups, the result will be less talking and working together and therefore less gains on measures of learning. These connections between classroom management and learning gains have been documented in two separate years of data collection on complex instruction (Cohen et al., 1989).

Avoid rushing to the rescue at the first sign of difficulty in a group. Force the group back on its own resources by refusing to answer questions unless the entire group has been consulted for possible answers. Many teachers have a rule that only the facilitator can ask a question after having made sure that no one in the group has the answer. In moving about the classroom, make a conscious effort not to look as if you are an available member of the group.

While the Groups Work

Students are now doing many of the things you ordinarily do—like answering each other's questions, keeping each other engaged in the task, helping each other to get started. After teachers discover that they do not appear to be needed because everything is running without them, they often say, "I feel like I've been done out of my job; it all works without me. What am I supposed to be doing?"

Despite the ability of groups to carry on by themselves, your role is not one of *laissez-faire*. You are now free for a much higher level and more demanding kind of teacher role. You now have a chance to observe students carefully and to listen to the discussion from a discreet distance. You can ask key questions to stimulate a group that is operating at too low a level; you can provide feedback to individuals and to groups; you can stimulate their thinking; you can look for low status behavior and intervene in order to treat for status problems; and you can reinforce rules, roles, and norms in those particular groups where the system is not operating at its best.

There is a delicate balance between avoiding hovering and wisely intervening in a group. The price to be paid for intervention is reducing interaction within the group. Ask yourself whether you are willing to pay that price. Although groups should be allowed to make mistakes for themselves, there are times when nothing is to be gained from letting a group struggle onward:

- When the group is hopelessly off-task
- When the group does not seem to understand enough to get started or to carry out the task
- When the group is experiencing sharp interpersonal conflict
- When the group is falling apart because they cannot organize themselves to get the task done.

Don't rush in at the first sign of trouble. Stand close enough to hear but far enough away so that your presence is unobtrusive. Carefully listen and make an hypothesis about just what kind of problem the group is experiencing. Are low status students being shut out of the group? Is it a problem of group process? Is it some inability to understand the directions? Is it a problem of how to proceed? Is it a lack of background, academic skills, or content knowledge? Perhaps you will decide after watching and listening that the group will solve its own problems and does not need you.

If you decide to move in, what you do or say depends on your hypothesis about what the problem is.

- A group is having trouble getting organized. You remind them of the rules and roles. You ask whether people are playing their roles. You suggest that the facilitator discuss what they have to get done, make a list, and help the group to prioritize what needs to be done first and who can do it. You tell the group that you will be back to hear the results of their discussion. You then leave.
- A group has "gotten stuck" on a problem and doesn't seem to be getting anywhere. The level of frustration is rising. You ask a few open-ended questions in an attempt to redirect the group discussion. You suggest that the group deal with your questions in their own deliberations—and you walk off.
- A group is not sharing materials cooperatively. You could ask them to stop for a few moments and talk over how they are doing on some of the cooperative norms (ideally, posted somewhere in the room). Then you can ask them to tell you after having had a brief discussion what their conclusions are and what they think they should do about it. (Don't stay to supervise the discussion.)
- A group is struggling with a difficult text and does not know how to analyze the document. They are in need of some intellectual assistance. You point out some of the key parts. You check for their understanding of what is being asked. You may even fill them in on missing parts of their knowledge. This does not mean you are doing the task for them or directing them how to do it. You are merely moving them to the point where they can cope with the demands of the task.
- A group of second graders has plunged into the task without reading instructions. You tell the group that you don't want

them to touch the materials until they can tell you just what they are supposed to be doing. You say that you are going to return to the group and ask any member to explain what it is they are supposed to be doing. If that person can explain, then they can get started with the materials. Otherwise, they will have to continue to read and discuss.

In none of these examples are you using direct supervision. Instead, you are using the system of roles and norms to make the groups operate. You are forcing the group back upon its own resources—to take more responsibility for its own learning and functioning.

In addition to these cases of groups experiencing severe difficulties, you may want to intervene in order to deepen the thinking on the assigned topic. Asking questions is an excellent way to achieve this end provided you do not stay around to answer your own questions or to call on various group members to guess what you have in mind. Without giving an answer, the teacher can help students to analyze a phenomenon or a problem in terms of its parts and interrelationships. For example, a group of students in science are having problems making a flashlight. The teacher responds by saying, "Not everyone's flashlight is working. Have you tested each part of it to see if it's working? By sharing with each other the parts you find that work, you might be able to figure out how to get it working." Questions beginning with "why" are good for stimulating analytic thinking. You might ask a group of students working on the Crusades, "Why did the Crusaders try to dehumanize the enemy?"

Your attention will also be necessary if one group finishes their work very quickly while the others need more time. You might open up the task once more by asking some questions about analyzing the problem further, or about generalizing the task to another situation. For example, you might ask: What other ways are there of . . . ? How can we use what we learned in . . . ? Do you think this is true of all . . . ? What would happen if you did things another way? You might also ask the group to consult reference works that you have provided to extend their activity and their thinking.

Management of Conflict

Disagreement about ideas is a healthy sign during groupwork as long as intellectual disagreement does not degenerate into sharp interpersonal conflict. Some interpersonal conflict is inevitable and should not be taken as a sign of failure. Nor should it be an opportunity for you to intervene and take over the reins immediately, acting as arbiter, juror, and judge.

What can you do? Ask the group what seems to be the difficulty. Then ask them to think of some alternative strategies for handling the conflict. If you have prepared your class with strategies for conflict resolution, as described in Chapter 4, they will be able to envision alternative ways to behave. If you have really delegated authority, then the group should take responsibility for solving its interpersonal problems. Even younger students are able to develop workable strategies for managing conflict when challenged to do so and when the teacher persists in demanding that they talk things through until they find a solution.

If the problem is due to a volatile combination of students, make a note not to put that combination together again. Changing the composition of groups on a regular basis and rotation of roles will help to defuse interpersonal problems so that the conflict does not become chronic. If, however, you think you are seeing the same problem in a number of groups, there may be a difficulty with the way you have prepared the students and/or the nature of the task. Take the time to have a whole class discussion during wrap-up and see if you can locate the general problem. Be prepared to make adjustments in your task, to do some retraining and reinforcing of rules and roles, or to develop some strategies with the class as a whole that will solve the problem.

Holding Students Accountable

Teachers are anxious to grade groupwork and to use systems of points for acceptable behavior because they know that it is important to hold individuals and groups accountable. However, these strategies are unnecessary in the management system just described. There are multiple alternatives in the system you can use for this purpose. When you intervene while the groups are working and require the group to pull itself together and function, you are holding the groups accountable.

You also hold the group accountable by requiring a presentation of their work during the wrap-up phase. When a group has failed to work together well and has not addressed the questions raised on the activity card, they need to know that you are aware of what has happened and expect them to do better in the future. You may choose to deliver this feedback to the group while they are still working at learning stations and reserve your more general commentary on what is to be learned from their experience for the rest of the class during wrap-up. For example, you could point out that the next group to do this task should be sure to work with the omitted discussion questions. If, however, you start a round of applause for every group performance no matter how weak, the students will realize that there is no group accountability in the system.

By providing feedback to groups on their group process, you can show that you intend groups to take responsibility for what happens while they are at work. Simultaneously, you can confirm their accomplishments, recommend effective strategies they employed to other groups, or point out the difficulties that will require some attention. Feedback on group process can take place while the group is working or during wrap-up. While helping the groups to learn more effective strategies, your feedback also has the function of letting the students know that you are watching their behavior very carefully and holding them accountable for what happens in their groups.

Individual accountability is maintained by reading over the individual reports or products. If individuals find that you do not know whether or not they have completed a group report or if they are pretty sure you never read these documents, they may become "free riders" in their groups.

Teacher's Role for Orientation and Wrap-up

During orientation you are clearly in direct charge of the students. Their job is to listen and to ask questions if they do not understand. This does not mean that a long lecture is in order. I often stand at the back of the classroom while teachers give orientations and usually note that students have difficulty paying close attention to what the teacher is saying. Even in high school, they seem to "tune out" after five minutes. Those teachers who use visual aids and who involve the students in a discussion concerning what they are about to experience are much more successful in holding the class's attention than those who attempt to tell everything that the students will need to know.

During wrap-up the teacher listens carefully to group reports, providing feedback and stimulating discussion. Asking higher order questions at this time will encourage students' thinking. Following student presentations, the teacher would do well to comment on what has been learned from the exercise. It is necessary to make connections between the activities and the central concepts they are supposed to illustrate. Otherwise, students get lost in the interesting and concrete details of their group products and forget the point of the lesson.

Wrap-up is also the time to provide feedback on what you observed while students were at work in their groups. If you constantly interrupt to provide feedback while they are in groups, you will run the risk of "hovering" and reducing the interaction. Many teachers find that it is better to circulate among the groups, listening and taking notes on a clipboard. Then, during wrap-up or during the orientation the next day, they provide feedback to groups and individuals. Feedback, under these circumstances, has the double function of holding groups accountable and of helping the students with their understanding of the intellectual tasks at hand. It is a priceless opportunity to offer public praise to students who have done very well in the context of groupwork—particularly those who are not high achievers in conventional academic tasks.

WORKING AS A TEAM

One of the most gratifying experiences for a teacher is to plan and carry out groupwork designs with a trusted colleague. Just as students use each other as resources in groupwork, teachers can do the same. With the joint wealth of past experience as to what tasks work well with students and as to how instructions can be made clear, teachers can be highly creative as they work together. They can also provide honest and constructive feedback as ideas develop.

When instruction is complex, as is the case with groupwork, having teachers work together means that they are able to be of great assistance to each other while the class is operating. Perhaps one teacher can stop to work with a group needing intervention, while another keeps an eye on the classroom as a whole. One teacher can prepare the orientation while another can do the wrap-up. The labor of preparing complex materials for learning stations can also be divided.

Another advantage of a colleague is the benefit that accrues when two or more teachers hold formal, scheduled meetings. In these meetings (even if they are as short as twenty minutes) one has a chance to consider various problems that have come up, to raise possible alternatives, to choose one, and to talk once more in the next meeting about how good or bad the decision was. This kind of thoughtful and evaluative decision making is very difficult to carry out all by oneself. In research with teachers, Intili and I have repeatedly found that teachers who hold regular team meetings are better able to implement complex and sophisticated instruction than those who rely on brief huddles just before and during class (Intili, 1977; Cohen & Intili, 1982).

The last major advantage of working with a colleague lies in having someone to make an observation and systematic evaluation of your groupwork in progress. It is almost impossible to run groupwork and evaluate what is happening at the same time. Chapter 9 includes a number of simple techniques for a colleague to use in helping to evaluate your groupwork. Even beginning teachers can provide helpful feedback using these techniques. And you can return the favor by observing in your colleague's classroom.

Finding Ways to Team

There are two kinds of teaming; one requires more organizational change than the other. The first kind is joint teaching where your colleague actually teaches jointly with you in your classroom. I use the word "colleague" because this person does not necessarily have to be another classroom teacher. I have worked with successful teams made up of a resource teacher working with a classroom teacher for one period a day, a teacher and an aide, or a teacher and a trained parent volunteer. If your class is difficult to control and unused to groupwork, you will need another person, especially at the beginning. If your tasks are complex—such as using different science experiments at different learning stations, or working with sophisticated equipment like video cameras—and if you have different groups of young students doing very different tasks, another person becomes a necessity. This is as true for classrooms as it is for any other organization: Complex technology is more effective when staff work more closely together (Perrow, 1961).

If you have a friend on the faculty with whom you would like to try some of these groupwork activities, talk to the principal about finding ways to work together. If a large room such as a multipurpose room is free, it is possible to combine two classes for the actual groupwork. If the classes are from different grades or if you are combining with a class for special education, you will be surprised to see how well students of different ages and levels of academic achievement can work together in this setting. If you are combining age groups, it is especially important to pick a task that older students can extend and develop, but also one that younger students will be able to manage with assistance. It will also be necessary to include special training to show students how to help other people without doing each other's work.

If you decide to work with an aide or a volunteer, take the time to train that person as to your expectations of them during the teaching process. If you do not train them, the result will be that they will move in and try to supervise groups directly. Aides or volunteers can become valuable colleagues if you allow them to bring in suggestions and to make evaluations of what is happening. In these circumstances, you are still the decision maker; it is the role of your assistant to observe and gather data about what the problems are during the course of groupwork. You also expect that they will make constructive suggestions during team meetings.

If you cannot manage joint teaching, the next best thing is teaming for planning and evaluation purposes. It is not difficult to find the time for brief meetings with a colleague for planning purposes. In addition, you need to find time for that colleague to visit your classroom and time when you can return the favor. It is during these visits that the evaluation devices can be used. Following evaluation, a meeting should take place to discuss the results of the evaluation and to decide what should be done in order to improve the procedures. Most principals are supportive of this type of collegial effort to improve instruction. Some principals even volunteer to take over classes for an hour while the visits are going on. I have worked at very few schools where the teachers and administrators were unable to work out a suitable plan.

Collegial interaction of this sort is highly rewarding. Evaluations of in-service programs requiring this kind of collegial interaction have consistently revealed that teachers find working with a colleague in planning, observation, and evaluation one of the most satisfying and stimulating of their professional experiences. Despite initial doubts about having another teacher watch them at work, they find that constructive criticism from a colleague who is facing the same kind of practical classroom problems is helpful; they realize that they have wanted and needed this kind of feedback for a long time.

8 Treating Expectations for Competence

It is time now to return to the dilemma of groupwork discussed in Chapter 3. What have we done about the problem of high status students dominating interaction and of low status students withdrawing from the group? There is an even more fundamental question: Have we done anything to change low expectations for competence, the underlying cause of nonparticipation by low status students?

Recall that high status students are generally expected to do well on new intellectual tasks and low status students are generally expected to do poorly on these same tasks. When the teacher assigns a groupwork task, general expectations come into play and produce a self-fulfilling prophecy in which the high status students talk more and become more influential than the low status students. The net result of the interaction is that the low status students are once again seen as incompetent. This occurs even if groups are given a rich new task that does not stress ordinary academic skills.

Two strategies will have some impact on this problem: (1) establishing cooperative norms such as "everyone participates" and "everyone helps"; and (2) giving every student a part or role to play. Both of these strategies will raise participation rates of both low and high status students and will prevent high status students from doing all the talking. Furthermore, low status students, just by talking and working together, will improve their performance.

Doesn't that take care of the whole status problem? Not exactly—nothing has happened to change expectations for competence. Imagine a well-trained group with different students playing different roles; the low status students are doing just as much talking, on the average, as the high status students. Nevertheless, members of the group still think of the low status student as having fewer and poorer ideas than the high status students. The low status students may be active, but they are still less influential and less active than the high status students. And the low status students still feel that their contributions to the group are less valuable and less competent than the contributions of the high status students. Furthermore, in moving from the successful group experience to other groupwork tasks, there is no improvement in expectations for competence.

In order to produce active behavior in low status students that will be perceived as competent, and in order to produce expectations for competence that will transfer to other tasks, something must be done to change the nature of those expectations for competence. They are too uniform, and too consistently negative. It is necessary to create some positive expectations for intellectual competence that will combine with the preexisting set of negative expectations.

If you are successful in attacking the problem of consistently low expectations, students who have been unsuccessful in your classroom can acquire a sense of competence that will be acknowledged by their classmates. As you proceed to different groupwork tasks, students can expect themselves and can be expected by classmates to make good contributions to each new assignment.

MAKING A LOW STATUS STUDENT THE GROUP EXPERT

One obvious way to change low expectations for competence is to design a situation where the student who is expected to be incompetent will actually function as an expert. The simplest and probably the safest way to do this is to find a task where the student is already an expert. An example might be a Spanish-speaking student who could teach classmates a song or a poem in Spanish. Even this fairly obvious strategy requires careful analysis. Do not assume that because a student has a

Spanish surname or speaks some Spanish, he or she knows how to teach something in Spanish. Proficiency in Spanish may be limited; in addition, teaching someone else is a separate skill from knowing how to recite a poem or sing a song. You must prepare the student carefully for this teaching role.

Speaking in Spanish is a kind of expertise that everyone, rightly or wrongly, expects Hispanic students to have. This is a narrow and specific expectation for competence, almost like a stereotype. It is unlikely that the experience of being an expert in Spanish will change expectations for competence on other kinds of tasks because it is a stereotypic expectation associated with ethnicity. A similar situation would be a female who demonstrates expertise in cooking or an African-American who demonstrates expertise in basketball. Although people are willing to grant females and African-Americans expertise in these two areas, the expectations for competence *do not transfer* to other valued tasks.

Despite these limitations, a narrow brand of expertise has some merit if it gives the low status child a chance to play the leadership role of teacher. However, unless you point out to the class that the act of teaching the class is a special kind of competence and that it is an important skill, the group will never notice that "teaching the Spanish song" is a different skill from "singing the song."

Every student in your class is an expert in some valued intellectual skill. Try and find out what these are. Rich groupwork tasks allow you to see skills and talents that ordinary classroom assignments never permit. Some classrooms have a list of the areas in which each student in the class is listed as an expert. Take note of areas of expertise and find ways to allow different children, particularly those with low academic, social, or peer status to function as experts in a group. This simple technique is workable as long as the members actually believe that the student is an expert and as long as the student is truly competent.

EXPECTATION TRAINING

Along with graduate students and colleagues, I have carried out a number of experiments where expectations were treated by having the low status student become a teacher of a high status student on a new, challenging, and valued task. This method of treatment is called "Expectation Training." Tasks for expectation training are not culturally specific or stereotyped for any group. We have used tasks like constructing a model from straws based on a mathematical law, building a two-transistor radio, or solving a plastic Chinese puzzle.

The strength of the treatment lies in the way that it attacks expectations for competence held by the low status student for himself as well as those held by the high status student for the low status student's performance. Theoretically, making low status students experts on a new task and making them teachers of that task provides two new sources of positive expectations for competence. The students derive positive expectations from displaying competence on the task itself; in addition, they derive expectations for competence from being successful teachers. These new expectations combine with the older set of negative expectations; the net effect is to raise the general level of expectations for competence. The result is improved participation and influence on new group tasks.

In laboratory settings, expectation training has consistently produced an increase in participation and influence of children with low social status; treated groups exhibit a pattern of equal status behavior. The treatment has worked for African-American–white groups (Cohen & Roper, 1972); for Chicano–Anglo groups (Robbins, 1977); for Canadian Indian–Anglo groups (Cook, 1974); and for Western and Eastern Jews in Israel (Cohen & Sharan, 1980).

In a field experiment with an interracial summer school, we were able to show that if expectation training were used the first week, it was possible to maintain equal status interaction for six weeks. African-American students taught white students a series of academic and nonacademic tasks. For this purpose, the African-Americans came to the summer school a week early for special training in their role as teachers. At the end of the program, African-Americans were as active and influential, if not more active and influential, than the whites on the standard group task of Shoot the Moon (Cohen, Lockheed, & Lohman, 1976). The African-American students were from a markedly lower social class than the white students in this field study. (All were fifth and sixth graders.) However, in the summer school setting the curriculum did not require conventional school skills as a prerequisite to success on tasks in the curriculum.

Expectation training is an extraordinarily powerful treatment. The low status student not only displays an impressive competence, but is in a position to direct the behavior of the high status student as does every teacher—a rare opportunity for someone on the bottom of the classroom status order. Even with a nonacademic task (such as a Chinese puzzle) for expectation training, the favorable evaluations received as a puzzle solver and as a teacher will transfer to a wide variety of groupwork tasks requiring intellectual skills.

Expectation training should never be undertaken without serious thought and should not be tried at all if the teacher does not have the resources (aides, older students, volunteers) to spend time with each low status student who will play the role of teacher. The danger is that if you allow the low status student to *fail* as a teacher, you will have knowingly exposed that student to another overwhelming negative evaluation. *This must not be allowed to happen.* The only way to avoid it is careful individualized coaching, so that you are sure that the student is highly confident and can demonstrate his or her competence to the trainer's satisfaction before going on to teach.

Expectation training is not the most practical of classroom treatments. Teachers often do not have the time to prepare students for their role as teacher so that a successful performance is guaranteed. Even if an aide is assigned this task, the aide will need to be carefully trained so that each student reaches some specific criterion level of competence before any demonstration of teaching skills takes place.

One of the most difficult things to achieve in this or any other kind of status treatment is to convince the low status persons of their competence. It is actually harder to change expectations these students hold for themselves than it is to change expectations classmates hold for them. You may observe that low status students can carry out the task and teach it with considerable skill. But you would be surprised to realize that these students still do not see themselves as skillful.

Another important problem may arise in having the aide do the training. If the teacher belongs to a high status ethnic or racial group, and the aide belongs to the same minority group as the low status students, expectation training may be ineffective. Experimental results have shown that expectation training will *not* produce the desired effects in settings where the adults mirror the status order of the outside society, for example in a classroom where an Anglo teacher is the "boss" and a Hispanic aide is clearly a subordinate. Unless the aide and the teacher model equal status behavior, the low status student is unlikely to speak up and tell the high status student what to do (Cohen, 1982).

THE MULTIPLE ABILITY STRATEGY

"As you see people working together, you see all of the abilities that other students have that you didn't see before. There was this one kid, and he was really shy. He was always, like out of everything. He was never doing something or speaking out until we had an art project we had to do and he—like he just *visualized,* just got a pencil and piece of paper and like acted and draw a lot things that people didn't even see in him until that one time that we saw another part of him." (Maria, a seventh grade student)

Maria is a student in a classroom where the teacher has been using a multiple ability treatment for status problems. Maria does not see her fellow students ranged along a dimension from "smart" to "dumb." She sees people as having multiple intellectual abilities, and groupwork as an opportunity to find out about those special abilities.

Furthermore, Maria realizes that the groupwork tasks her teacher assigns require many different intellectual abilities, skills, and competencies. Because the teacher has said many times: "None of us has all of these abilities. Each one of us has some of these abilities," Maria expects at the beginning of a new task that each student will have something valuable to contribute and that no one student will know it all. As a result, she and other group members are prepared to listen to contributions from each group member and are less willing to sit back and let one person do most of the contributing.

The effectiveness of this treatment lies in altering the set of expectations with which students start on a new task. Instead of uniformly high expectations, high status students are expected to show strengths and weaknesses like everyone else. The same is true for low status students who are now expected and expect themselves to be good at some of the important abilities relevant to this task. The teacher has created a *mixed set of expectations* for everyone. Thus, when the students work together, the differences in expectations for competence between high and low status students are much smaller than in classrooms where teachers do not use such a status treatment.

Research Evidence

The multiple ability treatment was developed by J. Tammivaara (1982) in a laboratory study of students selected on the basis of having high and average estimates of their own reading ability. Her treatment consisted of explaining the different abilities necessary for a survival task of Lost on the Moon (see Hall, 1971) before the groups began their discussions. The host experimenter said: "No one person will be good at all these abilities, but each person will be good on at least one" (p. 216). Furthermore, students were told that reading had no relevance to this particular task since all the objects were pictured on cards. Those groups that had heard the multiple ability introduction showed equal status behaviors, while those who had not heard such an introduction exhibited a pattern of dominance by the high ability readers. This study demonstrated that one can effectively interfere with status processes by defining multiple abilities as relevant to a task, thereby preventing students from assuming that academic status will be the only relevant basis for predictions of competence.

Rosenholtz (1985) created a one-week multiple ability curriculum for classrooms of fourth graders who had known each other for some time and who had many opportunities to make evaluations of each other on reading ability. In this classroom experiment, Rosenholtz created a mixed set of expectations, not by telling the students about abilities but by having them experience three new abilities in the context of small groups each supervised by an adult. The three new abilities were: visual thinking, reasoning, and intuitive thinking. Group tasks were carefully engineered so that high ability readers could not dominate and low ability readers would gain more favorable evaluations of their competence. This was accomplished by having students take turns at guessing the answers and by using tasks where everyone contributed something different to the final product. Groups were recomposed between tasks, so students worked with a wide variety of their classmates.

On the standard game of Shoot the Moon, the results showed that low ability readers who had experienced the curriculum were significantly more active and influential on the new task than the low ability readers from an untreated class. Behavior did not truly equal status in treated groups in that there was still a tendency for high ability readers to be more active and influential. But the advantage of the high ability readers was greatly reduced by the treatment.

The multiple abilities curriculum provided low status students with the opportunity to develop favorable self-evaluations and to be evaluated favorably by peers in the context of tasks defined as requiring new and different abilities—tasks where division of labor and turn-taking prevented status phenomena from operating. Once the favorable evaluations had been formed, they combined with the old set of expectations for competence and modified the status effects on a new and different task.

In multilingual, academically heterogeneous classrooms where small groups were working on discovery tasks in math and science, I had already demonstrated strong status effects (Cohen, 1984). When teachers used a multiple ability status treatment for this same setting, similar to that used by Tammivaara, effects of status on interaction were reduced, though not eliminated (Cohen, Lotan, & Catanzarite, 1990). High status individuals were still more likely to offer assistance than low status individuals, suggesting that status was associated with expectations for higher levels of competence.

What Are Multiple Abilities?

Use of the multiple abilities strategy means thinking in a new way about human intelligence. Instead of thinking about how intelligent or unintelligent a student is, imagine that there are different kinds of intelligence or intellectual abilities that are called forth in different kinds of situations and for different aspects of a given task. Take, for example, the task of teaching. Teaching requires great interpersonal intelligence, organizational ability, conventional academic ability, verbal ability, as well as creative ability.

When we think about the adult world of work, it is comparatively easy to see that many different kinds of abilities are essential to any job such as that of teaching. Yet somehow when we think about intelligence among students, we automatically narrow to conventional academic criteria—being good at reading, writing, and computing. That narrowness is, in part, a reflection of the narrowness of school curricula. Instead of reflecting the way adults use their minds, school curricula reflect a traditional conceptualization of what is to be learned in school.

The narrowness of conventional academic tasks is one of the features of classrooms that helps to create a unidimensional status order, where students rank each other on one dimension of ability. One is either good, average, or "no good" at school tasks. Furthermore, one of the earliest indicators of the child's academic ability is his or her ability in reading. Reading ability becomes an index of general intelligence in many classrooms for both students and teachers.

The multiple ability approach is in line with current work on reconceptualizing human intelligence. For a long time human intelligence has been thought of as unidimensional; it could be characterized by a single number; people (and whole races) could be ranked from gifted to stupid. Stephen Jay Gould in his important book, *The Mismeasure of Man* (1981), has done the field of education a great service by tracing the history of this idea to its roots, deep in Western culture. His analysis of biases present in early and present-day research on the concept of intelligence raises fundamental doubts as to whether we can continue to think of intelligence as unidimensional. Howard Gardner in his book, *Frames of Mind* (1983), attempts to reconceptualize human intelligence as multiple and rooted in specific areas of the brain; he distinguishes linguistic, musical, logical–mathematical, spatial, bodily-kinesthetic, and personal intelligences. Sternberg (1985) sees intelligence as a set of processes that individuals bring to bear on situations with which they are faced. For Sternberg, intelligence is both multidimensional and eminently trainable.

The multiple ability treatment requires you to convince the students that many different intellectual abilities are necessary for the groupwork tasks. Before you can do this, however, you must analyze those tasks in terms of the abilities required. There is no official list of multiple abilities. It is a new way of looking at something we have known all along—that we use our intelligence in many different kinds of ways to solve problems and to accomplish important tasks in work and family life. Keep in mind that adults engage in highly complex problem solving as part of their daily lives. Some of these activities are academic, others are technical, political, and many are interpersonal, social tasks. Examples of such adult activities are managing, coordinating, taking the role of the other, teaching, learning, researching, directing, supervising, writing, drawing, building, developing, investigating, negotiating, evaluating, counting, calculating, and acting. These are all activities you can find in rich groupwork tasks.

If we could think about students in the same way we think about ourselves as adults, each with strengths and weaknesses on all the abilities required by living and working, many of the status problems I have described would disappear. Thinking in this way does not require that each person be labeled as having particular special abilities and therefore not allowed to develop new abilities. Rather, I recommend thinking about intellectual abilities as *specific and relevant* to particular activities, so that any particular person can be shown to have many different useful abilities. Students should have the opportunities to try out a wide variety of activities, so that they can continue to develop their intellectual abilities.

Steps of a Multiple Abilities Strategy

There are two steps to a successful multiple abilities strategy: (1) Convincing the students that many different abilities are required for the task; (2) Creating a mixed set of expectations for each student.

The best time to use this treatment is during an orientation to groupwork. You can convince your students that many different abilities are required through your own analysis of the assigned tasks. Suggest some of the *specific* intellectual abilities or skills that you think these tasks require. Ask students to suggest abilities or skills that they think will be required. Point out how these abilities are useful for adult problem-solving situations. During the wrap-up point out which of the multiple abilities that were identified during the orientation were used while completing tasks at the learning stations. You could ask students to share additional abilities that turned out to be critical. Students like Maria quickly learn how to analyze tasks and to think in this new way for themselves.

Some students may have excellent reasoning ability. You will want to talk about this general ability in a very specific way, more in the way we talk about skills. For example, solving a problem experimentally, hypothesizing, logically analyzing the problem, figuring out how something works mechanically, analyzing an issue from various perspectives, or making connections between ideas and concepts are all specific ways to describe how reasoning is required by particular groupwork tasks. Instead of describing students in general terms as creative, you could talk about creating a dramatic role for a skit, generating multiple alternatives, thinking of new uses for familiar objects, composing a song, conceiving of an idea for an illustration, imagining what it must have been like to live a long time ago, or taking the role of another person very different from oneself. Many of the rich groupwork tasks I have described require spatial and visual ability. Again, to be more specific, you might talk about diagramming mathematical concepts, drawing an idea as a cartoon, creating a model, or seeing how a sophisticated mechanism can be constructed.

The second step is the one teachers most often omit, but it is critical. After explaining that these tasks call for many different abilities, always include the following statements: *None of us has all these abilities; Each one of us has some of these abilities.* Help students see why this is likely to be true. If the tasks are truly multiple tasks, it is most unlikely that any one person will be outstanding in all the required abilities. And surely each student will be able to make an intellectual contribution in some way. These words are the heart of the multiple ability treatment because they help students to see that there is no such thing as being good or bad at groupwork but that the most sensible position is to hold mixed expectations for competence. Teachers who are highly skilled in using this treatment often state that for the best possible group product, it will be necessary for students to recognize and use everyone's abilities.

Do's and Don'ts of Successful Treatments

Focus on abilities that students see as intellectual. Students value but do not see social skills as intellectual abilities. Unless you can convince students that there is such a thing as social intelligence, don't refer to an "ability to get along with others" as one of the multiple abilities.

Avoid talk about abilities that suggests that some students are good with their heads while others are good with their hands. Western culture does not view work with the hands as intellectual work. The same is true for the work of the artist. When discussing artistic ability, break it down in terms of the task in the way that Maria did: visualizing or creating a design or using artistic symbols.

Be very specific about how these abilities are important for particular tasks. Encourage students to analyze necessary abilities for themselves. Also, encourage students to develop new abilities. Don't imply that people only have inborn abilities.

The Multiple Ability Curriculum

Obviously, you cannot use the multiple ability treatment unless the groupwork tasks actually require multiple intellectual abilities. These are the rich groupwork tasks I described in Chapter 5. If the groupwork assignments are ordinary classroom seatwork, then the students will never believe that many different abilities are required.

Tasks that require students to create a role play, build a model, draw a mind map of the relationship between ideas, or discover and describe relationships through manipulating equipment or objects, are examples of multiple ability tasks. Students can discuss challenging questions prior to or as part of creating a final group product. Science tasks are easily seen as requiring multiple abilities such as observation, precise manipulation, careful data recording, hypothesizing causes and effects, and writing up the report clearly and concisely. Two examples from other subject matters may be helpful:

- A teacher of advanced German in high school who wants to further students' understanding of the German subjunctive voice, asks the groups to create their ideal world. The final product "Unsere ideale Welt" must represent the collective opinions of the groups. They have to represent their ideal world in a picture and present it to the rest of the class, talking about it in the subjunctive voice. All discussion must be in German. Each group has art supplies, a German–English dictionary, and the activity card. (Anneliese Ohlund, Los Altos High School, Los Altos, California, 1992)
- A middle school English class is studying *The Martian Chronicles* by Ray Bradbury. Among the culminating group activities designed by teacher Jean Babb is a dramatization of one of the stories using a Reader's Theater format. Typically in Reader's Theater actors dress alike, use music stands to hold script, and arrange themselves on the stage in a meaningful way. Scripts are read. Voice and gesture become very important in conveying characterization to the audience. A second group is asked to select a story and stage an investigative news show. A third group is asked to stage a talk show about one of the stories and a fourth group is asked to produce a skit. (Jean Babb, Jane Lathrop Stanford Middle School, Palo Alto, California)

Reading, Writing, and Calculating

Basic skills are part of multiple ability tasks. For example, someone has to be able to read the activity card. Everyone has to write an individual report, even if it is only a sentence in the case of a young child. Arithmetic operations are often part and parcel of interesting groupwork task.

However, basic skills are not a prerequisite for successful participation in the task. Weak readers can receive assistance from group members. They can listen to the group discussion of what is involved. They can interpret pictures and diagrams on activity cards. Weak writers will be motivated to express their own ideas after participating in the creation of group products that employ central concepts. They can receive peer assistance in expressing their own ideas. They may also be motivated to write about ideas they have contributed or heard in the group discussion.

In the multiple ability orientation, you and the students will undoubtedly list basic skills as required for the task. Since they are only part of the required set, they will be seen as important but will not, as in many traditional classrooms, have the power to make some students who are weak in these areas feel as if they cannot do well in the activity.

ASSIGNING COMPETENCE TO LOW STATUS STUDENTS

Candida Graves, a fourth grade teacher of a bilingual class-room describes what happened when she assigned competence to a low status student:

"One day I had a student named Juan. He was extremely quiet and hardly ever spoke. He was not particularly aca-demically successful and didn't have a good school record. He had just been in the country for two or three years and spoke just enough English to be an LEP student. I didn't notice that he had many friends, but not many enemies ei-ther. Not that much attention was paid to him.

We were doing an activity that involved decimal points

and I was going around and noticed he was the only one out of his group that had all the right answers. I was able to say, 'Juan! You have figured out all of this worksheet correctly. You understand how decimals work. You really understand that kind of notation. Can you explain it to your group? I'll be back in a minute to see how you did.' And I left. I couldn't believe it; he was actually explaining it to all the others. I didn't have faith it was going to work, but in fact he explained it so well that all of the others understood it and were applying it to their worksheets. They were excited about it. So then I made it public among the whole class, and from then on they began calling him 'the smart one.' This spread to the area where he lived, and even today kids from there will come tell me about the smart one, Juan. I thought, 'All of this started with a little intervention!'" (Candida Graves, Rose School, Milpitas, California; Graves & Graves, 1991, p. 14)

Once you have set the stage with the multiple ability strategy, assigning competence to low status students is a second treatment you can use to modify expectations. This treatment takes advantage of the power of the teacher as an evaluator. Students tend to believe evaluations teachers make of them. Thus, if the teacher publicly evaluates a low status student as being strong on a particular multiple ability, that student will tend to believe the evaluation. The other students who overhear are also likely to accept the evaluation's validity. Once the evaluation has been accepted, expectations for competence for this task are likely to result in increased activity and influence of the low status student. Success at this task will translate into success in future groupwork tasks as it did in the case of Juan.

This is a very powerful treatment. It can do much to boost the participation of a low status student. Ordinarily you may only watch low status students to see if they are confused or staying out of trouble. You and the other students in the group may not even notice when the low status student does something really well. To assign competence you must observe when the low status students actually do make intellectual contributions. It is a good idea to carry a clipboard while students perform groupwork. This enables you to record your observation of what the low status students are doing.

An effective assignment of competence has three critical features:

- Evaluations must be public
- The evaluations must be specific, referring to particular intellectual abilities/skills
- The abilities/skills of the low status student must be made relevant to the group task.

Public recognition of competence is a key factor. Assigning competence is not simply a treatment for the low status student—it is a group treatment; the problem lies partly in the expectations that others have for the low status student. Therefore the group's expectations for this student must also be changed. Public recognition means that you are making it known that you think this student is competent on a particular skill/ability. This helps to change the student's expectations and the expectations held by classmates for this student.

As students move into the middle school, there is a danger that too much fuss over any single student will cause embarrassment to the student and possible sanction from peers. Just state in a matter-of-fact way what you are actually observing about his or her skills; don't gush. Be honest; don't make up stories about the student's abilities that you didn't actually see. Also, you don't have to reserve this treatment only for the lowest status students in the class. There are many students from the middle to the lower ranges of the status structure who would greatly benefit by your evaluation.

If you are very specific about the ability or skill the student is exhibiting, the student and the entire group will know exactly what he or she did well. It is not hard to be specific if you, like Candida Graves, speak in concrete terms about skills like understanding a notation system on a particular mathematics assignment.

Finally, making the ability relevant to the task has the effect of making the improved expectations for competence especially strong for the current activity. To make the ability relevant teachers often say, "Rosita is an important resource for this group. She can help you with putting together your tangrams" (or whatever skill or ability you are discussing with respect to the task).

This is not an easy treatment to carry out. It requires you to observe students in terms of performance on multiple abilities. It also requires you to analyze what they are doing so that you are specific and so that you can make the ability relevant to the task. Many teachers find that it is easier to take notes while students are in their groups and present the assignments of competence the next day when they have had a chance to think and to study their notes in peace and quiet. Assignments of competence can be combined in an orientation with feedback to the groups on yesterday's cooperation and performance.

The more frequently teachers use the multiple ability treatment and assign competence, the higher the participation rate of low status students in elementary classrooms (Cohen, 1988). In classrooms where teachers used these treatments more frequently, there was less difference between participation of high and low status students than in classrooms where teachers used these treatments less often.

THE MULTIPLE ABILITY CLASSROOM

These strategies for treating status problems are highly recommended for groupwork. They will increase engagement and participation of low status students. They will improve expectations for competence in a way that will transfer to new and different group tasks. There is no reason, however, to expect newly acquired favorable expectations for competence to transfer to reading and math lessons conducted in a traditional fashion. If you use ability groups and if these lessons use only a narrow range of skills, you can quickly reconstruct a status order. If you stress competitive marking and grading as the major form of feedback for students, you will also aggravate status problems.

With some changes in tasks and evaluation practices and with proper treatment of status problems, you can create a multiple ability classroom. Such a classroom has many dimensions of intellectual competence. No one student is likely to be rated highly on all these dimensions. Each individual is likely to be rated highly on at least one dimension. Thus, there are no students who are generally expected to be superior regardless of the nature of the task.

To create a multiple ability classroom, use more multiple ability tasks featuring higher order thinking and integrating basic skills. Students can be temporarily grouped for instruction for specific basic skills that they lack. As long as students see math or reading as requiring a variety of skills and abilities, you can avoid reconstructing a status order. Talking to students specifically about their performance can be combined with conventional marking and grading so that individuals are well aware of their strengths and weaknesses on multiple dimensions. These changes enable you to teach at a high level despite great diversity in academic skills.

9 Evaluating Your Engineering

Kathy Egan and Debbie Marsing worked as a team on the first day of groupwork in Ms. Egan's secondary school swimming class. Students were assigned to work in pairs on developing the whip kick for the breast stroke. Students were supposed to help each other by analyzing each other's stroke and by making suggestions for improvement. The task was defined as requiring multiple abilities such as observation skills, ability to analyze your partner's movement, understanding your partner, coordination, strength, and endurance. Ms. Marsing evaluated the groupwork by making general observations, by watching several students whom Ms. Egan had pointed out as having had problems in the class, and by giving the students a simple questionnaire to fill out. Ms. Marsing wrote:

> The instructions to the students were clear. Kathy explained the different tasks involved especially well. Kathy took approximately five to seven minutes to explain the different abilities involved in the task, as well as how the students should work together. She had a chalkboard with abilities listed and the helper and doer roles that corresponded to that ability.
>
> In the actual activity, the students in Group 2 had trouble getting started. They were the least involved in the beginning. Both students commented that they knew the breast stroke perfectly. When they began to teach and learn the breast stroke from each other, both students were engaged. . . . Another pair, Ray and Rick, were on task during most of class time. During the five minute observation, it appeared that Ray and Rick were working together; however, minimal verbal interchange was heard. They did not deliberate much, but Ray would swim ahead as the doer and Rick would watch. When Ray got back a couple of words may have been spoken, but then Rick would be on his way, swimming,

this time with Ray watching. . . . Ray had some trouble communicating because of his lack of English proficiency. . . . Ray often used his hands to help describe the whip kick to Rick; Rick, who had the worst whip kick, was being helped by Ray, who had a good kick. Here, the lower status student was much needed for his movement and observation skills. He was doing well on these skills notwithstanding his weak English speaking skills.

Based on their performances, it appears that students didn't completely understand the procedure of helping and teaching each other. Gradually, they understood by watching other groups perform the team task. I didn't see the weaker students stand out any more than the others during the class. This also relates back to the third item on the questionnaire. The students who *did* understand were both high and low status students. Also, the students who *didn't* understand were high and low status students. Even though some students were primarily the helper or doer, the source of this domination was a function of the students' movement skills rather than their relative status. Those with better skills were helping those who were less skilled. (Egan & Marsing, 1984, pp. 2, 3, 5, 6)

As a result of this evaluation, the teaching team realized that analyzing someone else's performance in swimming was a skill that required special preparation before groupwork begins. Next year Ms. Egan will have this critical piece of information available in her notes when she begins to schedule activities in preparation for groupwork next year.

Be critical of your groupwork the first time you try it. Even if you have faithfully adhered to the general principles for designing groupwork, principles do not fit concrete situations without adjustment. Even with the best laid plans, there is room for improvement.

Teachers who have designed groupwork carefully are typically so delighted at the capacity of student groups to run themselves on the first trial that they are in no mood to be critical. However, it is extremely important to examine the very first day of operation with an objective eye. Some problems can be observed and corrected quickly; others may require revising the initial instructions or making other structural changes in the way the task is handled. Even if it is too late to correct a problem in a class you are conducting, careful notes will allow you to improve the design for the next class. If, as recommended, you have found a partner who can work with you in planning and evaluation, you can rely on your partner's observation to provide the needed objectivity.

TOOLS FOR EVALUATION

Some effective and simple tools to use in evaluating your own groupwork are provided below and in Appendix B. These have been developed in classrooms and do not require special training in data collection or analysis. Practicing teachers and beginning teachers have found them practical and useful. Included within this chapter are a sample observation guide and a participation scoring sheet; a sample student questionnaire, along with a guide for analyzing it, is included in Appendix B. The sections below will describe all these forms and how to use them. Depending upon which aspects concern you the most, they may be used separately or together. Undoubtedly you have a number of concerns: Will the students be fully engaged with the groupwork? How well will I be able to play my role? Will the students be able to cooperate? How well will the low status students do? Go over the various instruments and select parts or specific questions of concern. It is more important to focus on a few important aspects of evaluation than to do a superficial job with all possible aspects.

Guide for an Outside Observer

I am assuming that you will have done some of the initial planning with a partner and that you have arranged for this partner to visit your classroom on the day you plan to start the groupwork. You have discussed with your partner what you are trying to do, what the problems are, and which students may require special attention. As a result, the plan for evaluation is a joint decision about what and whom to look at.

While the students start to work in their groups, the observer can move around the room watching and listening. If you point out to the observer the students you are most concerned about, she or he can observe their behaviors carefully. These may be low status students, students who lack English proficiency, domineering students, or students who usually present behavior problems. The observer can also watch you in action.

Figure 9.1 presents a Sample Guide for the Observing Teacher. Using these guidelines, the observer can take notes. These are possible questions for the observer. You should go over this guide with the observer in the planning session, picking out which questions you want to include. You may want to add a few others.

Part A focuses on the teacher's orientation. It is particularly important for the observer to arrive in time to see and hear you at this stage. So many problems start with confusion in the orientation. On the other hand, in an effort to make all the details clear, the teacher risks losing the attention of the students by trying to get across too much information in a lecture format.

Part B directs the observer's attention to the groups at work. A good procedure is to look over the whole classroom and count how many students are wandering, unattached to any group, and how many students are waiting for the teacher. The observer should scan the classroom and try to determine how many of the groups seem to be at work on their tasks in the way in which they were supposed to work (Questions 1 and 2). Then the observer can move around to stand near enough to each group to hear and see, but not so near that students become conscious of being observed. Questions 3–7 in Part B should be considered for each group. A seating plan with the groups numbered can enable the observer to share observations on particular groups with the teacher.

Part C has to do with selected students who are seen as problematic in the groupwork setting. It is important to spend about five minutes with each of these students taking notes on the questions for each one.

Part D deals with you, the teacher. The first three questions are on common problems that teachers have when they first start groupwork: hovering over groups in a way that inhibits their interaction; spending too much time trying to keep students on task instead of letting the groups take responsibility;

and spending too much time trying to get the students through the task instead of letting the group members help each other.

Even if you do manage to avoid these problems, your chief concern may be the mechanics of getting everyone through the task. Particularly at first, it is very difficult to give good feedback to the groups and to ask them stimulating questions to encourage their thinking. This skill may only come with sufficient time and practice. Don't be disappointed if you are not able to play this part of your role at first. The next two questions deal with those aspects of your role. Be sure that the observer takes sufficient time to watch you in action so as to get a fair picture. The last question concerns your use of the status treatment of assigning competence. If you are carrying out this treatment properly, an observer should hear you making a specific and public evaluation of a student's competence.

Use of a Student Questionnaire

If the students are at least fourth graders, many important questions can be answered with a questionnaire. If all the students do not read well, you can read the items out loud. A Sample Student Questionnaire is included in Appendix B. These are questions that have been very successful with children as young as nine years. These particular items allow you to examine the success of low status students. By asking students to put down their names on the questionnaire, you can pick out the students of special interest and see whether they reported participating. You can actually see if any low status students were picked as having the best ideas or were chosen as having done the most or least talking in the group. There is usually a good relationship between students' reports of such matters and systematic scoring of an observer.

If you have used a multiple ability strategy, then students should be able to list an ability on which they thought they did well. Also, they should be able to list some of the abilities you introduced in addition to reading and writing.

Even the success of the training in cooperative norms can be checked with a student questionnaire. Do they report experiencing problems with not being listened to or with talking much

FIGURE 9.1: Sample Guide for the Observing Teacher

A. ORIENTATION

1. How clear are the instructions?

2. Does the instructor make use of visual aids and discussion rather than lecturing?

3. How attentive are the students to the orientation?

4. Is the assignment of facilitator and other roles clear? Do the students know who the facilitators are and what they are supposed to do?

5. Does the instructor make clear that people have the right to ask group members for help—and that group members have the duty to assist others?

6. Is the assignment of students to groups and the locations for groups carried out quickly and efficiently?

7. *For Multiple Ability Tasks*: Does the instructor make explicit the multiple abilities involved in the task? Does he or she make clear that reading and writing are only two of the abilities involved in the task? Does he or she make clear that everyone will be good on at least one of the abilities?

B. STUDENTS AT WORK IN THEIR GROUPS

Overview

1. How many students are wandering around, not part of a group? How many students are waiting for the teacher?

2. How many of the groups are engaged in their task? Are there any groups where students are working individually rather than as part of the group?

Group by Group

3. Are the students confused about what they are supposed to do? If so, is the group functioning to solve the problem?

4. *For classes that have received training in cooperation*: Make a list of the cooperative norms included in the training. Do you see evidence of these norms in operation? Do you see situations where the students are failing to observe these cooperative norms? Describe.

5. *For groupwork with specific roles*: Make a list of roles and the expected behaviors. For each role, can you hear and see someone

playing this role in the group? Are there any roles that are not in evidence? Is the facilitator (if there is one) dominating the group?

6. Do you see any evidence of conflict? Describe.

7. Is any one student dominating a group? Is there one student who is saying very little?

C. SELECTED STUDENTS

The teacher should point out the students he or she wants observed, so that observer can take notes on what is happening to particular students. Prepare a list of these students, and take notes on what is happening to each one.

1. Do some of the weaker students show a grasp of the problem? If they are having difficulty, is someone helping them?

2. Are low status students participating? Is anyone listening to them? If they are supposed to be playing a role, are they doing so?

D. THE TEACHER

1. Is the teacher hovering over the groups and not allowing them to figure out things for themselves?

2. Is the teacher spending most of the time getting students back on task?

3. Is the teacher spending most of the time trying to help the students with how to do their assignment?

4. When a group or a student has a question, does the teacher try to get the group to solve the problem for themselves?

5. Is the teacher stimulating thinking with specific feedback and questions?

6. Did the teacher assign competence?

The observer should go through each of the above parts systematically, taking notes in answer to each question that is applicable after spending some time observing the groups, the students, and the teacher.

less than they wanted to? Did people have trouble getting along in the group? Would they be willing to work with this group again? You should pick and choose questions according to your major concerns. You can make up additional questions.

A Guide to Analyzing the Student Questionnaire is also included in Appendix B. The directions should be self-explanatory. This guide is divided by the kinds of questions teachers want answered about their groupwork. Data analyses are suggested that will provide some answers to each question.

Systematic Interaction Scoring

An alternative to the questionnaire method is systematic participation scoring by an outside observer. This is much less difficult than it sounds. It is relatively easy to obtain a rough estimate of the rates of participation of different students. The observer can spend some time writing down answers to the questions you have provided in the Guide for the Observing Teacher; in a fifty-minute session, there will also be time to do some systematic scoring. In any case, it will be important for you to have everything ready and to have instructed your observer ahead of time in the procedures you want.

Select the "target students" you want to have observed. These may be any or all of the following: students with low academic status; students who tend to dominate; minority students who have little social influence among their classmates; very quiet and nonparticipating students; students with limited English proficiency; and/or students who present special behavioral problems. Next, make out a scoring sheet, such as that shown in Figure 9.2, in which you draw the location of the various groups around the classroom, with a box to represent each student in each group. Point out the location of the target student within the group when the observer is ready to score. Have the observer label the boxes in each group to represent the target students.

The observer should spend at least five minutes scoring each group. I am assuming that there will be five or six groups with four or five students each. The observer simply makes a hatch mark inside the appropriate box for every speech a stu-

FIGURE 9.2: Sample Participation Scoring Sheet

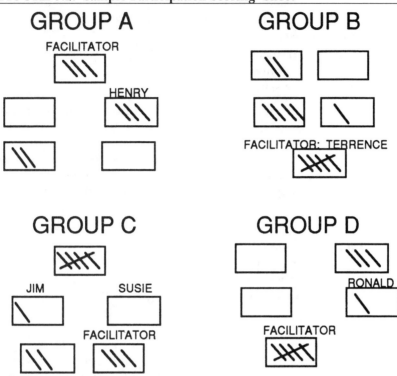

dent makes relevant to the assignment. That speech can be as short as "OK," or it can run for several minutes. A speech ends when the person stops talking, starts talk that is social or unrelated to the task, or is interrupted by another speaker. It is important to record the contribution of the target student. Sometimes errors will be caused by members of the group moving around and in and out of the group. Try not to let this happen for the target student. If the target student moves away from the group and ceases participating, it should be so noted. The observer has to stand close enough to the group to hear and see, but not so close as to make the students aware of what he or she is doing.

The tabulation and analysis of these data are very simple (see Figure 9.3). How many of the low status target students

FIGURE 9.3: Sample Participation Scoring Calculations

How many of the nonparticipants in the class (i.e., students who never talked) were low status students?

a. Total nonparticipants	6
b. Low status nonparticipants	1
Percentage low status ($a \div b \times 100$)	17%

Conclusion: Very few of the nonparticipants were low status students.

How did the rate of target students' participation compare with the average rate of their group? (Sample calculation given here is for Group A; calculations for other groups should be made in the same manner.)

	Target Students	Other Students
Number of students	1	4
Total number of speeches	3	5
Average speeches per student	3	1.25

Conclusion: Henry talked more than average for his group.

were never seen participating? How many students in the whole class were never seen participating? If the low status target students make up half or more of the nonparticipating students, you are observing a status problem. More precise calculations can be made by examining the number of times the target students were scored in comparison to the number of times other people in their group were scored. The simplest way to do this is to compare the average number of speeches of target students to the average number of speeches for other members of their group (see the second sample calculation in Figure 9.3).

Then compare the target students' figures to the average figure for the group. Are they below average? Are most of the target students below average in their respective groups? If the groupwork task has been effective in moderating status effects, some target students should be below average, some close to average, and some above. This method of scoring also allows you to tell at a glance if some member of a group is dominating the group by talking far more than anyone else. If you are concerned that your facilitators are doing too much of the talking, have the observer note the facilitators on the chart so that you can examine their rate of speaking in comparison to the average rate of other members of the group.

The figures for any single target student should be viewed with caution because it may well be that the particular five minutes that the group was being scored were not representative of the group's pattern of interaction as a whole. This method of scoring has the advantage of objectivity but the disadvantage of allowing only limited conclusions to be drawn from the numbers. The questionnaire has the advantage of richness of the inferences that can be drawn but the disadvantage of the subjectivity of the responses.

IMPROVING THE GROUPWORK

Schedule a conference with your partner. Congratulate yourself on how well things have gone. What are the major problems that have been identified? These are the agenda items for your conference, and you should take time to think about possible solutions in advance. If your groupwork is ongoing, some of the solutions can be put into practice immediately. Start with the questions identified in the planning session for the evaluation. For example, if you were concerned with the clarity of your instructions, then check all the data you have on this point. After pulling together everything that has been learned from the evaluation, including the systematic data and your own rough observations, come to some conclusions about how the next session of groupwork could be improved. It is very important to do this in a systematic fashion. Your conference will be much more effective if you force yourself to come to some decisions in light of what you have learned. What has gone very well and can be left alone? What needs some adjustment and what do you and your partner think should be done about it? Write down these decisions and file them along with your instructional plans for the groupwork task. If you do not do this, it is too easy to forget what you have learned and to return to reliance on a vague overall judgment of how it went. You are not a good observer when you are trying to do something new and difficult like introducing and running groupwork. Furthermore, there is not much point to going through the motions of a systematic evaluation if you do not pay attention to the data and use it to make decisions.

What can you do if you carry out a status analysis and conclude that you still have a marked status problem, with some students doing most of the work and low status students offering very little to the group? Go back to Chapter 8 and see if there are some techniques you can introduce. Perhaps you need to spend more time with a multiple ability introduction. Perhaps you should observe low status students during groupwork and find a way to assign competence to those students. Perhaps you need to introduce a facilitator role to make sure that everyone participates; and perhaps if the low status students are encouraged to play this role, they will receive a much-needed boost in expectations for competence.

A teacher cannot become a full-time evaluator. Obviously one has to pick a practical method of evaluation. It makes sense to try one of these techniques at a time. As you gain experience, it takes much less time to analyze the data. If you are attempting to treat a particular problem you have identified from the first round of evaluation and you want to evaluate the second round to see if things have improved, be sure to use the same instruments the second time. When you have tried out the new solutions and evaluated them, you will have a tested groupwork format that you and your partner and any other colleagues can use. You will be surprised to find that a carefully thought out and evaluated design will work well with a wide variety of classes; the students will respond with enthusiasm and excitement year after year.

10 Groupwork in the Bilingual Classroom

The dedicated classroom teacher of a bilingual or an English as a Second Language (ESL) classroom faces a scene of enormous complexity—linguistic, academic, and cultural. At the same time as the teacher struggles to help the children understand what is to be done in each assignment, he or she is trying to improve language proficiency and often to remediate basic skills. Furthermore, there are such differences in what each child will need to understand instruction and to make reasonable progress that conventional methods of ability grouping do not really simplify the situation. If teachers group children by language proficiency (as has been recommended by the federal government), what do they do with the academic differences? And if they group by academic ability, how can they be sure that everyone understands the language of instruction?

I am not a specialist in bilingual education, but for the past 14 years I have worked with teachers in elementary classrooms where the issue of language is a central one. Early in this work, I discovered that it was not a clear-cut issue of whether the child was Spanish speaking, English speaking, or proficiently bilingual. Very often we find children who do not test as proficient in either English *or* Spanish. The actual linguistic status of such children is not well understood.

Furthermore, the issues of social class and of culture are thoroughly mixed with the issue of language. Some of these children with limited or minimal English and Spanish come from very poor economic conditions; they are arriving at school with the strengths of their own culture but without many of the preschool experiences that prepare children for the typical curriculum. Also from low income homes are some children who have

experienced no schooling; it is not uncommon to find new immigrants of eight or nine years of age who have never before
been in school.

Many third-, fourth-, and fifth-grade bilingual classrooms
contain children with minimal skills in reading and writing any
language; some of these students started school with limited English proficiency. They had no access to instruction in a language they could understand; as a result they have not made
good academic progress. For those students with proficiency in
Spanish but with limited English proficiency, it would seem clear
that instruction in the mother tongue in these basic skill areas is
critical to insure academic progress. Many of the classrooms that
I have been privileged to work with have proficient bilingual
teachers and teaching materials in both languages. Children in
these settings have the major advantage of having access to the
language of instruction.

To make the scene even more complicated, there are other
non-English languages in the schools. With Asian immigrants
come a variety of languages such as Laotian and various Viet-
namese dialects. Often it is not possible to find in the classroom
another child, credentialed teacher, or trained aide who knows
the language of the newcomer. These children are typically
placed in ESL classes where the top priority is to learn English
quickly, sometimes to the neglect of the other academic subjects.

Most commonly, the school's major goals for bilingual and
ESL classes are to increase linguistic proficiency in English and
to move students up to grade level in basic skills. The mistaken
assumption is made that English is a prerequisite to instruction
in the basic skills (Cummins, 1979). Emphasis on teaching of
English is often at the expense of challenging instruction in the
basic skills. As a consequence, the students fall further behind in
content while learning the new language.

Groupwork offers a powerful tool for the attainment of both
English and basic skills. At the same time, it can be used to enable teachers of such classrooms to provide access to higher order thinking skills. This chapter will start with the issue of oral
proficiency and will move to the problem of presenting the
grade-level curriculum to a class that is heterogeneous academically and linguistically. The final section will illustrate how

groupwork can be used to produce broad-gauge achievement results with a bilingual approach designed to develop thinking skills.

ORAL PROFICIENCY

In a review of the research literature on how children acquire a second language, McLaughlin (1985) finds that second-language learning is accelerated when learners have meaningful interaction with peers who are native speakers of the language. The idea of native speakers as language models is not new in second-language pedagogy. However, common school practices work against peer interaction between English-speaking and limited-English-speaking children. In the first place, limited-English-speaking children are often removed from the regular classroom and placed in special classrooms either for bilingual instruction or for ESL. Certainly in this setting where they are isolated and stigmatized, they are unlikely to have significant peer interactions with English-speaking classmates. Secondly, within classrooms where there are proficient English speakers, even when cooperative learning is employed, one often finds the Spanish speakers segregated in their own small group.

Today there is a growing number of two-way bilingual immersion programs (Lindholm & Aclan, 1991) demonstrating that where children are instructed in both languages and where the teachers make frequent use of mixed-language groups in cooperative learning, all the students become bilingual. In addition, these children perform very well academically when assessed on standardized tests in both English *and* Spanish.

Krashen (1988) argues that the second language learner must experience "comprehensible input," meaning language instruction that is a bit beyond the learner's current level of proficiency. Simple immersion in an English-speaking group does not present comprehensible input if the child is not ready for such an experience. Further, comprehensible input must be provided in a context that does not evoke anxiety in the limited-English-proficient child. Krashen discusses a number of ways in which comprehensible input can be organized in the classroom and in the playground. In groupwork situations that provide nonverbal cues and context from manipulative materials or charades, for example, interaction between peers may be a very effective way of providing comprehensible input while also instructing on content.

According to Faltis and Merino (1992), the learner speaks and listens in interactions in which it is necessary to communicate. If teachers are skilled communicators, they give clear directions for classroom tasks, structure those tasks so as to require participation, and use classroom materials that enhance meaningful student participation. In this way comprehensible input is provided in an interesting and nonthreatening atmosphere which fosters successful second language learning in much the same way as first language develops.

The language of teaching is especially critical when children are limited-English speakers. Academic activities that require interaction to learn content are preferable to direct language instruction (Cazden, 1988).

These recommendations are very similar to what I have called "rich tasks for groupwork." Particularly if training and the organization of the groupwork have insured that everyone must participate, it would seem that the stage is set for the optimal conditions that the experts recommend.

Groupwork and the Development of Oral Proficiency

A kindergarten teacher who participated in research in her own classroom as part of the Teacher Investigator Project* was surprised at how easy it was to integrate groupwork into her teaching.

> It was so simple, we didn't realize that it was going to be that simple—we were assuming that it was going to be this tremendous, difficult, complicated thing—and it really wasn't that hard at all. You could adapt a lot of tasks to work in those kinds of situations. So you can integrate normal daily things like reading and math.

*The Teacher Investigator Project was financed by the Anglo American Education fund and was conducted under the auspices of the Stanford University School of Education.

It don't have to be something you get out of an oral language development book. Once you learn how to give them independence, you can adapt things from the text.

This teacher's class presented typical problems of differences in linguistic proficiency. Many of the children at this school enter kindergarten with a limited vocabulary. Furthermore, this limited vocabulary may be divided between two languages. Some children with limited English proficiency are unwilling to speak in the classroom at all. As one of these children was described, "When he first came and you would ask 'What's your name?' he would just smile." Others in the same class have a good level of proficiency in either Spanish or English.

The issue for this teacher was: How do you get these children to talk? Do you try to teach them some more English through whole group activities such as drill and practice or through reading out loud to them? And what do you do with those who have a good grasp of English while you are working with those who do not?

With the help of the school's reading teacher, the teacher found that kindergartners given a pretraining program in activities such as Broken Circles that are designed to help them work as a group were then able to participate in many additional activities that stimulated lively discussions. Examples of such activities included giving each group a card with a new word on it and asking them to develop a charade portraying this word so that other groups could guess it. Here, those children who knew English acted as a valuable resource and explained the word to those who did not. Furthermore, everyone had ideas about how the charade should be carried out. In still another task, the reading teacher came to the room with paper pig ears and noses for each group. Their task was to enact "The Three Little Pigs." According to the teacher's report the children developed numerous adaptations of the original story with a good deal of excitement and maximum communication. This classroom teacher even found that simple tasks requiring visual memory could be adapted to group discussion. She gave them a detailed drawing of an elephant followed by an elephant drawing with many details missing. Each child had to fill in the incomplete version, but they helped each other with the details, for example, "Pedro, you're missing the eye." Before the school year was over this teacher found it relatively easy to have one or two oral proficiency activities a day. Interestingly, when the teacher and the reading specialist compared tape recordings of a group of children discussing a live animal made before and after these experiences, they were pleased and gratified to find that almost all the children had increased dramatically in their willingness and ability to speak.

Group Composition and Linguistic Proficiency

If the task is rich with context, pictographs, and manipulatives, it is possible to place children who share no common language in the same group. Although it is still quite a struggle for the newcomer, if the group is trained to see that everyone gets the help needed, the children will do a remarkable job of communication.

If at all possible, mixed language groups are preferable. Otherwise the students will not have the benefit of hearing peers with English proficiency. When a child is monolingual in Spanish or in another language, he or she should be combined with English speakers and with a proficient bilingual child. The bilingual child needs to be taught that he or she is a valuable bridge in the group, explaining to the monolinguals what the others are saying and offering special help to the non-English-speaking students. It is also important for the English-speaking students to understand the contributions of the non-English speaker. In the classrooms where both languages were utilized by both teachers and children, Neves (1983) found that the bilingual children had, as a whole, the highest social status; they were most often chosen on a sociometric measure as friends and as good in math and science. As the year progresses in a bilingual classroom, one can often find children who can understand another language even though they cannot speak much of it as yet. My staff has often observed conversations between a Spanish- and an English-speaking child, each speaking in his or her own language, but clearly understanding the other.

In the Spanish–English bilingual classroom, sometimes

members of a group will speak in Spanish and sometimes they will speak in English. Our studies have shown that there is no need to enforce an English-only rule. English proficiency will develop in this context. If there are English monolinguals in the group, the rules of cooperation work against excluding the English speaker from understanding what the others are saying. By the same token the Spanish speaker will not be excluded in a predominantly English-speaking group.

GRADE-LEVEL CURRICULUM IN HETEROGENEOUS SETTINGS

Very often, by the time the limited-English-speaking students reach the fourth or fifth grade, they speak English in the classroom. However, while they were struggling to master the language, they missed instruction in the basic skills and so are functioning several years behind grade level. The most pressing problem experienced by the teacher is the need to remediate basic skills while moving ahead with the grade-level curriculum.

Once the students have been trained to work in groups, curricular tasks that are required for the grade level, tasks with many basic skill components, can be adapted for groupwork. Students who are more advanced can assist those who are less advanced. Students who are bilingual can assist those who do not understand the English text. From the fourth grade up, the new immigrant can receive excellent assistance because there are so many proficient bilingual students. The efficiency of the teacher is multiplied in this way because there are many "assistant teachers" who are making sure that everyone understands the instructions and the text of the assignment.

A fourth-grade teacher and a fifth-grade teacher I worked with in such settings found that they could teach Spanish and English grammar as well as skills of reading comprehension of a very high order by training their students to work in groups and by composing heterogeneous groups. The fifth-grade teacher reported that the students were able to work with eighth- and ninth-grade textbooks in science. She had the groups paraphrase several sentences for every two pages they

read. They had to recognize the topic sentence in each paragraph and to underline the key concepts. They used these key
concepts to make up their own table of contents for their version
of the material. This was a three-month assignment given to
groups. She reported that their work came back showing excellent comprehension. The students would help each other with
the reading and would then discuss how to complete the assignment. Students played roles of reader, recorder, and facilitator.
This is an excellent example of how groupwork can permit the
teacher of the heterogeneous classroom to teach to the highest
level and not to the lowest common denominator or even to the
average student.

FINDING OUT

Finding Out/Descubrimiento (De Avila & Duncan, 1980) is a set
of activity cards and worksheets designed to foster the development of thinking skills in second through fifth grades. All learning materials are presented in Spanish, English, and pictographs. The Program for Complex Instruction at Stanford
University has developed a system of classroom management
that is used in conjunction with these materials. In earlier chapters I have already described some of the key features of cooperative learning developed at Stanford for this instructional approach. Chapter 4 described the cooperative techniques used to
prepare heterogeneous groups to work at learning stations.
Each child is responsible for completing the task and worksheet,
but the group is responsible for seeing that everyone gets the
help he or she needs. Chapter 6 described the specific roles such
as facilitator, checker, and reporter that take over some of the
work of the teacher and insure that no one is left behind or
becomes disengaged.

In this chapter I would like to show how Finding Out and
the strategies of complex instruction contribute to the development of oral proficiency, acquisition and/or remediation of basic
skills, and development of grade-level concepts in math. However, the dramatic gains that we have seen with Finding Out
occur *only* when teachers and students receive adequate prepa-

ration for complex instruction that involves extensive training for cooperation, multiple roles for students at the learning stations, and delegation of authority by the teacher. The curriculum materials are marvelously engineered, but they are not magic. Unless children have proper access to each other as resources, and unless they are taught to solve problems as a group, many children will not understand what to do with the materials.

Materials and Management

Finding Out activities use the concepts of science and math to develop thinking skills. At each learning station are two activity cards, one in English and the other in Spanish. The cards tell the students what the activity is and ask them some key questions. There are many challenging words on these cards such as "perimeter," "latitude," and "hexagon." Clearly these words are beyond the reading level of most students in second- and third-grade classrooms, where many cannot read or write at all at the beginning of the school year. Cards have pictographs indicating the nature of the activity. There are also worksheets in Spanish and English for each child at the learning station. They often ask the child to describe what happened; they also ask: "Why do you think it happened?" They may require a child to estimate in advance how big something will be. Then they ask him or her to put down the results of actual measurement and how far off this was from the initial guess. In this way the worksheets require a high level of inference and skills such as estimation, while at the same time requiring basic skills such as reading, written expression, and computation.

Measuring, experimenting, constructing, estimating, hypothesizing, analyzing, and many other intellectual activities allow the child to develop strategies for problem solving. The Finding Out activities always involve interesting manipulable materials. They have been developed so that they do not assume that the child has had a rich set of preschool experiences that are relevant to math and science.

Key concepts, such as linear coordinates, are embedded in the activities. The child encounters linear coordinates repeatedly in different forms and at different stations. For example, at one station, students locate their homes on a map, using the coordinates. At another station they work with longitude and latitude on a globe. After repeated experience with these abstract ideas in different media, the child acquires a fundamental grasp of the idea that will transfer so that he or she will recognize it in new settings, including in an achievement test.

The group has many functions in this setting. In the first place it is essential to assure that all children have access to the task. Unless they get help in reading the activity card, many of the children will be unable to get the benefit of the activity. Other children who can read perfectly well may still have difficulty with figuring out how a balance scale works or with winding coils in the unit on electromagnetism. Students are supposed to ask each other for assistance; they have experienced specific cooperative exercises designed to internalize this behavior and the behavior of helping others without doing it for them (see Chapter 4). The facilitator is specifically taught to see to it that everyone gets the help that is needed. Both cooperation and the many assigned roles help to insure that each person benefits from the activity.

A second function of the group is to provide a forum where differences in ideas about what to do and about what good answers are can be shared and discussed. The instructions on the activity cards leave a good deal of uncertainty in many tasks. The members of the group have to employ trial and error and must share their results, either by showing each other or by discussion. Again, the children have practiced explaining to each other and showing each other how things work in special exercises (Chapter 4).

A third function of the group is to take care of the problems of children who tend to become frustrated or who often become disengaged. Instead of the teacher having to come around the room to the six learning stations to assist children who are slipping off task, the group functions to make sure that everyone is at work. The rule is: No one is done until everyone is done.

A fourth function of the group is to deal with the problem of linguistic differences. The bilingual child explains to the Spanish monolingual what the others are saying. By the same token, the English speakers are receiving input from the Spanish speakers. The child who lacks English proficiency is exposed to a rich language experience as he or she uses the vocabulary of the activity card in a situation with all the context and nonverbal cues needed for "comprehensible input." Instead of the teacher having to explain everything in both Spanish and English, the activity cards, the manipulative materials, and the linguistic resources of the group take care of this problem. Thus the child receives simultaneous instruction in language and content (Brinton, Snow, & Wesche, 1990).

At the start of each Finding Out session, the teacher gives a brief orientation, perhaps demonstrating the concepts from one of the most difficult stations in that unit. The orientation can be a lively demonstration using visual aids and involving active discussion with the students. The teacher is asked to include a multiple ability treatment with a discussion of different kinds of intellectual abilities that will be called for in this set of learning stations. As prescribed in Chapter 8, the teacher includes the motto that no one has all these abilities, but each one has some of these abilities. He or she may also talk about the classroom management system, emphasizing norms of cooperation or how she or he wants one of the roles played.

While the students are working at the learning stations, the teaching team (sometimes a teacher and an aide and sometimes two credentialed teachers) circulates around the room, taking care not to interfere with the process of talking and working together. Only the facilitator may be sent to a teacher to ask questions; and even then teachers ask the facilitator to make sure that no one in the group can answer the question. The management system functions to free teachers from spending most of their time keeping students on task and making sure that everyone understands the instructions. Instead of having to be everywhere at once as direct supervisors, they are supportive supervisors. This involves asking higher order questions, stimulating the children's thinking, extending their activities, and giving specific feedback to groups and individuals. Teachers are on the alert for the display of some of the multiple intellectual abilities such as reasoning, visual thinking, and preciseness, especially on the part of low status children. If a teacher observes a low status child performing one of the multiple abilities well, he or she takes time to assign competence to that student by saying specifically and publicly what she has observed so that the student and the group know precisely what was done well.

At the end of each session, there is a wrap-up. The reporter from each learning station may share what the group has discovered. A low status student may provide a special demonstration of what he or she has done at the learning station. The teacher may point out some difficulties that some of the groups are having with particular learning stations. At this point the teacher may undertake an explanation of a scientific concept. Or the teacher may discuss how cooperation and role-playing are proceeding.

The students experience this approach for approximately one hour a day, four days a week. They are repeatedly reading and writing in a context that is highly relevant and interesting for them. Even though they may have to accept help, they want to put their own words down on their worksheets. For example, when children see what happens to the kernel of corn held over a Bunsen burner in a test tube, they want to write down their own ideas about why it popped. In the course of exposure to the concepts, activities, and materials they are developing high-level problem-solving strategies that youngsters in bilingual classrooms rarely experience because everyone is so concerned about their limited English proficiency.

Achievement Results

Starting in 1979, the Program for Complex Instruction collected achievement data from children experiencing Finding Out and compared their scores in a fall and spring testing (early and late during the curriculum experience) to the gains expected in a nationally normed population. The children came largely from working-class backgrounds; many of them were attending predominantly Hispanic schools in different districts in the Bay Area of California.

In 1979, 253 students from nine classrooms in San Jose were given the Language Assessment Scales (De Avila & Duncan, 1977) early and late in the year. This is a measure of oral proficiency in English and Spanish that is widely used in the United States. Results showed highly significant gains in oral English proficiency on the part of those children who had started with limited or minimal proficiency in English. The students who gained in language the most dramatically were those who tested with minimal proficiency in *both* English and Spanish (De Avila, 1981). Neves (1983) observed a special set of these children with varying language proficiency and found that the more frequently the Spanish monolingual children were talking about the task, the larger were their gains in the English language. This was true even though these children were largely talking in Spanish, but one must remember that they were functioning in heterogeneous groups where English was being spoken.

In all three years that we have collected data on the Comprehensive Test of Basic Skills (CTBS, 1981), we have found highly significant gains in language arts, reading, and mathematics subtests. In 1983–84, the CTBS science test was employed for the first time, and it too showed significant gains. Comparing these gains to those expected in the normed population revealed that the students were gaining more than the national normed population in every subtest of the battery. Particularly striking were the big gains that occurred each year in such subtests as math concepts and applications, math computation, and reading comprehension.

Just as important as these broad-gauge achievement gains was the research that showed how these gains were connected to specific experiences in the classroom. For example, when we visited the classrooms and systematically counted the number of children who were engaged in talking or in talking and manipulating the materials, we found that the proportion so engaged was very closely related to the gains on the math concepts and applications subtest (Cohen et al., 1989). In other words, students whose teachers set the stage for more talking and working together had higher average gains on the section of the math test that dealt with concepts and problem solving. Groupwork is the ideal setting for fostering the grasp of abstract concepts.

In order to maximize the amount of talking and working together, it is necessary for the teacher to delegate authority.

When the students were at learning stations, we found that those teachers who were trying to help the children get through their tasks, giving direct instruction, asking many questions, and disciplining, had fewer students talking and working together (Cohen et al., 1989). Those teachers who had trained the children well and had some children keeping track of others and helping others complete the task had no need to move from group to group to keep the work going. Also, those teachers who used more small groups found that they did not have to run around the classroom trying to help everywhere; the groups were able to manage better on their own. Because the teacher did not have to do direct supervision, there was more interaction and thus more learning in those classrooms.

Cooperative training and the use of roles boosted everyone's interaction; these strategies also helped low status children gain access to the manipulatives and to understand the written materials. Frequent use of status treatments helped to boost the expectations for competence of low status students, leading to increased effort, activity, and influence among these children. As a result, low status children learned more than they would have without these special features of cooperative training, roles, and status treatments.

Where did the gains in language arts come from? A visit to a Finding Out classroom reveals many students who are studying the activity cards and worksheets, arguing about what they say and what they are supposed to be doing. Those classrooms that had a higher proportion of students reading and writing had higher gains in the test of reading comprehension. Students are reading and writing for a purpose and not as part of some seatwork exercise that does not make much sense to them.

In one second-grade classroom the teacher told the students every day, "Don't touch the materials until you discuss what the activity card says and can tell me what you are supposed to be doing. I am going to come around and ask one of you to tell me what you are going to do." She would do exactly that, often asking nonreaders what they were planning to do with the materials. If the child could not explain, she would say, "I think you are going to have to read and discuss some more. I'll be back to see if you have figured it out." Navarrete (1985) made videotapes of groups at work in this classroom. She found that much of the discussion among the children centered on figuring out what the activity card said. The more frequently children sought help, received help, and returned to their task (what Navarrete calls a complete problem-solving sequence), the greater were their gains in reading comprehension. Nonreaders were stimulated to find out for themselves what the activity card said because they were anxious to move on to the interesting manipulable materials. In this way the teacher was able to produce gains in basic skills at the same time as her class registered major gains in the understanding of math concepts.

CONCLUSION

Because educators have such an overwhelming concern with language acquisition, the curriculum for students with limited English proficiency is often so narrow that it limits the students' intellectual development. In addition, the overwhelming emphasis on language can make both students and teachers self-conscious about language usage. Groupwork is an alternative approach that puts language in a useful perspective; language serves as communication in order to accomplish various learning objectives. For example, in complex instruction, people talk about challenging concepts because they want to understand, to communicate with peers, and to learn how to solve problems. Language is used in a meaningful context. It is used to describe, analyze, hypothesize, and infer. Moreover, insofar as possible, children have access to a language that they can understand.

In classrooms where children ordinarily score around the thirtieth percentile in the fall, the achievement results of using Finding Out are impressive. What can we learn from this experience? Mainly I think we should remember that these results came about as a consequence of carefully designed, theoretically sound learning materials, and as a consequence of hard work on the part of the volunteer teaching teams. Starting in 1982 the implementation was much more consistent from classroom to classroom, and the achievement results were correspondingly stronger. This was a consequence of a two-week workshop for teachers, and of a classroom management system using cooperative groups that was carefully researched and implemented. Finally, these results came about as a result of extensive support for the classroom teachers by school personnel and our staff. Each teacher ideally had three sessions with a staff developer based on as many as nine systematic observations of her classroom. Without all this, the results would not have been as consistent and powerful.

What if you have no access to such a high-power approach? You can still put many of the central principles used in the curriculum of Finding Out and in complex instruction to work. You can put language into its proper perspective as a tool of communication in a group that is trying to learn something worthwhile. You can use talking and working together to teach concepts. You can implement the classroom management system of cooperative norms and roles. You can create classroom learning stations by adapting from recommended activities in texts; you can create activity cards (preferably in two languages) for cooperative activities that have been published or are exchanged by teachers. You can teach students how to help each other across language barriers. You can provide situations that are rich in comprehensible input and opportunities to converse with peers. You can show students how to use each other as resources so that classrooms with students who are behind grade level need not be deprived of grade-level curriculum or of higher level thinking skills.

In fifteen years of work with teachers and with classroom research, I have found nothing so gratifying as the sight of language minority students working excitedly in groups, learning how to solve difficult intellectual problems for themselves. It is my hope that you who teach such students will decide to design a setting where you too can watch young scholars talking and learning together.

APPENDIX A

Cooperative Training Exercises

Making Students Sensitive to Needs of Others in a Group

BROKEN CIRCLES

The instructions to the participants and suggested discussion given below are those of the developers of Broken Circles, Nancy and Ted Graves (Graves & Graves, 1985). Broken Circles is based on The Broken Squares game invented by Dr. Alex Bavelas (1973).

The class is divided into groups of 3–6 persons. Each person is given an envelope with different pieces of the circle. The goal is for each person to put together a complete circle. In order for this goal to be reached, there must be some exchange of pieces. Group members are not allowed to talk or to take pieces from someone else's envelope. They are allowed only to give away their pieces (one at a time).

Instructions to the participants

Each of you will be given an envelope containing two or three pieces of a puzzle, but don't open it until I say so. The object of this exercise is to put these pieces together in such a way that each member of your group ends up with a complete circle. There are a few rules to make the exercise more fun.

1. This exercise must be played in complete silence. No talking.
2. You may not point or signal to other players with your hands in any way.
3. Each player must put together his or her own circle. No one else may show a player how to do it or do it for him or her.
4. This is an exercise in giving. You may not take a piece from another player, but you may *give* your pieces, one at a time, to

any other members of your group, and other group members may give pieces to you. You may not place a piece in another person's puzzle; players must complete only their own puzzles. Instead, hand the piece to the other player, or place it beside the other pieces in front of him or her.

Now you may take the pieces out of your envelope and place them in front of you, colored side up. This is a group task, and you will have 10 minutes to make your circles.

Remember, the task is not finished until each of you at your table has a completed circle in front of you. When all of you have finished, raise your hands. (If one group finishes before the others, suggest that they try to discover if there are any *other* ways they could put the pieces together to form different circles.)

Discussion

When all groups have completed the task or the allotted time has ended, the teacher should help the participants to identify some of the important things that happened, analyze why they happened, and generalize to other group learning situations. The following questions can serve as a guide to the discussion:

What do you think this game was all about?
How do you feel about what happened in your group today?
What things did you do in your group that helped you to be successful in solving the problem?
What things did you do that made it harder?
What could the groups do better in the future?

Help participants to be concrete about what they did and also abstract about the general implications of what they did and the lessons they learned for the future. In Advanced Broken Circles, one player may block the task for the rest of the group by completing his or her circle satisfactorily, but refusing to share some pieces with the others. This is analogous to a member of a cooperative learning group who tries to work alone and does not help other members.

In the discussion be sure to come back to the two key behaviors that make a group successful: *Pay attention to what other group members need. No one is done til everyone is done.* Point out when groups report these kinds of behaviors or when they decide that these behaviors will help them to do better in the future.

Directions for making and using Broken Circles are given below.

FIGURE A.1: Simplest Broken Circles

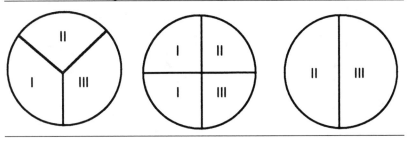

FIGURE A.2: Simple Broken Circles

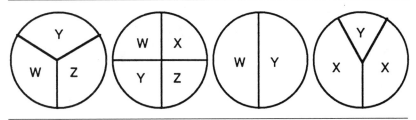

Directions for three levels of difficulty are presented. You may wish to use the intermediate and advanced versions, going on to the advanced version later in the year if you feel that this particular lesson needs to be reviewed.

Patterns to use for different age students

Simplest Broken Circles.   This pattern is suitable for children 5–7 years old in groups of three. Sort the pieces into three envelopes (I, II, and III, as marked in Figure A.1) and give one envelope to each player. Figure A.1 indicates one solution; in this solution each player must give up some of his or her pieces to other players. The diagram shows how pieces held by players I, II, and III can be rearranged to form three circles. Two circles composed of a half and two quarters represents an alternative solution.

Simple Broken Circles.   This pattern is suitable for children 8–10 years old in groups of four. Sort the pieces into four envelopes marked W, X, Y, and Z. Figure A.2 indicates one solution. Ask the groups that

FIGURE A.3: Advanced Broken Circles

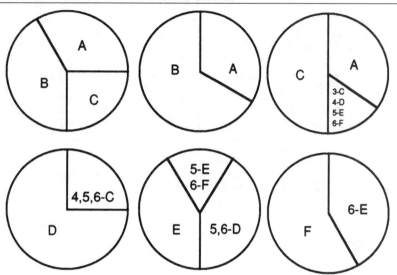

finish first, "How many *other* ways of forming four circles can you discover?"

Advanced Broken Circles.   This pattern is suitable for children 8–10 years old who have had some experience with Simple Broken Circles. It may also be used as a first exercise with older children, high school students, and adults.

Figure A.3 shows patterns for Advanced Broken Circles. A single set consists of fifteen pieces that will make six circles, as shown in the figure. Make one set of six circles for each small group. In Figure A.3, the placement of four pieces varies with the size of the group. For example, if you are playing with six-person groups, the piece marked 6-F goes into the F envelope and the 6-E piece goes into the E envelope, the 6-C piece into the C envelope and the 6-D piece into the D envelope. Repeat this pattern for each six-person group.

Once you have sorted a group set into the lettered envelopes, put these envelopes into a larger one. You are now ready to hand out the materials to the small groups.

Although it is fairly easy, once you are familiar with the exercise, to modify on the spot a set of six circles for groups of five or less, it is easier to make up and label sets of varying sizes in advance. Then these can be quickly substituted when required.

Instructions for making a set of broken circles

The circles can be any size from that shown to about 20 cm. in diameter. However, all the circles within the set should be the same size. Each set of circles should be a different color. This way, each small group will be able to work with pieces that are all of the same color, and different from any other group's color. This will enable you to easily sort the pieces when you are preparing the materials for the exercise.

The easiest way to manufacture the materials for any of the exercises in this appendix is to enlarge the diagrams in the figures with a xerox machine to the desired size. Then use the enlargement to reproduce the patterns on sturdy card stock of different colors. You will want to retain the labels in the diagrams of the circles to indicate in which envelope each piece belongs.

JIGSAW PUZZLES

Pick out some simple jigsaw puzzles. Each group member has a bag with one quarter of the pieces (for a four-person group). They have to complete the puzzle without a picture of the product in front of them. They may talk, but the task cannot be completed without each individual contributing his or her share. One child may not take another's piece and do it for him or her. Hints and encouragement may be given, but all the members must do their own part.

Following this exercise, hold a discussion similar to that suggested for Broken Circles. Bring out how this will be useful during groupwork. Students will each have information and ideas that will help complete the tasks given to the group. By sharing this information and these insights with others, everyone will be able to benefit by learning more from the activity.

Preparing Students for Learning Stations with Individual Reports and Manipulable Materials

In order to work in this setting students will have to learn how to help and explain, to ask questions, and to give good answers. Master Designer and Guess My Rule are two exercises suggested for teaching new behaviors concerning helping and explaining. As the students ma-

FIGURE A.4: "Master Designer" Shapes

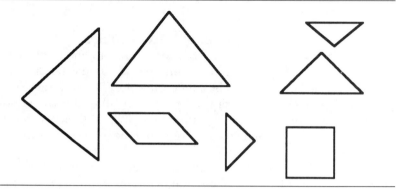

ture, it is very important to learn how to justify and give reasons for one's arguments as well as how to make one's thoughts clear to others. Rainbow Logic is included for this purpose. You may wish to develop your own using these as examples of how to pick out a situation that highlights and gives practice to new behaviors.

MASTER DESIGNER

Materials

This game requires a set of geometric shapes. Each player needs a complete set, but one person in each group takes the role of observer and does not require a set. A total of five persons per group is recommended, but smaller groups are acceptable. The shapes should be made out of some sturdy materials such as oaktag. The exact size of these shapes is given in Figure A.4. In addition, you will need some cardboard or other dividers that can be stood on a table. The idea is that each player can see the other members of the group over the divider but *cannot* see what the others are doing with their pieces.

Rules and discussion

One person plays the role of the master designer. This person has to instruct the other players as to how to replicate a design he or she has created with the pieces (all or part of them), but the master designer cannot do this task for them. Players cannot see what the others are doing, nor can they see the design of the master. However, group members may ask questions of the master designer. This illustrates an important new behavior:

Helping students do things for themselves

The group is dependent on the master designer for explaining how it should be done. This is the second new behavior:

Explain by telling how

In addition to verbal directions, students may use sign language to demonstrate to each other. This will help bridge any language differences you may have in your class.

When any member of the group feels that he or she has figured out the master design, the designer is asked to check the solution. If the master designer says it is correct, then that player too is to help others in the group by explaining how. This rule illustrates another important new behavior:

Everybody helps

Make up a bright chart with these three behaviors and display it prominently in the classroom.

After everyone in the group has completed the correct design, another student can take the role of the master designer. If you do not have time for everyone to take a turn, pick a variety of students to play this role—not just the natural leaders.

One student plays the role of observer for each round. The observer watches the group and checks off every time he or she sees two of the three new behaviors occur. These are

Explain by telling how
Everybody helps

Also make up a simple scoring sheet so the observer can check off new behaviors every time he or she sees them.

Since this is the first time students have ever been asked to observe, you will need to discuss how a person would know that a student is "telling how" and "helping others." It is not so important that the observer correctly record every time the behavior happens. The fact that someone is watching for and checking off behaviors helps to objectify behavior and will assist the whole group in recognizing such behaviors when they occur.

After the exercise ask each observer to report how many times he or she saw each new behavior. The observer may be able to give some good examples of what was seen. This provides an opportunity for the teacher to reinforce the new behaviors. Follow this with a discussion similar to the one described in detail for Broken Circles. Discuss how these behaviors will be useful for the curriculum. Explain that everyone will have to do his or her own report, so it will be important that everyone comes to understand and do things for themselves.

GUESS MY RULE

Objective

This is a game that Rosenholtz (1977) developed to illustrate reasoning skills. Students must deduce a central principle which accounts for all the different colored sizes and shapes that may be placed in the center of a ring. Someone holds a card, called a Rule Card, on which the central principle, such as "Only red shapes," is written. The rule card holder tells the players whether or not their choice of a playing card fits the rule.

Materials

Each group of five (three players, one rule card holder, and one observer) will need to have a set of rule cards, a large circle of yarn, and a special deck of playing cards. Each playing card displays one of four different shapes (circle, square, triangle, and diamond) in one of three sizes (large, medium, and small) and one of three colors (red, blue, and green); making up one card for each possible combination of shape, size, and color results in a deck of 36 cards. Outline the particular shape in the right size and color on the front of each card, and repeat the color on the border of the card. (It is much easier to draw the shapes on uniform card stock than it is to cut out cards in each shape, and the deck made with uniform cards is also much easier for the students to manipulate.) For each group of players you will also need to make up a set of rule cards. These are the cards with the central principle that the players must deduce. The rules are provided in Figure A.5.

Instructions to students

This reasoning game is called "Guess My Rule" and is played with this special deck of cards. As you can see, there are four different shapes in the deck: a circle, a square, a triangle, and a diamond. Each shape comes in three sizes: big, medium, and small. And each size in each shape comes in three different colors: red, blue, and green. There are many ways to sort these cards into categories. I want you each to think of a way. Here I have some rule cards that have on them different ways to sort the deck into various categories. The object of "Guess My Rule" is for you to try to reason out which rule card I am holding. We will put the playing cards in the center of the table, and you will each take turns picking one card. If the card you've picked fits my

FIGURE A.5: Rule Cards for "Guess My Rule"

1) Only △s

2) Only smallest shapes

3) Only BIGGEST ◇s

4) Only red* shapes

5) Only blue* ▭s

6) Only red* and blue* ◯s

* Outline these colors and shapes in the
  appropriate colors.

rule, I will say "yes," and you can put it in the yarn circle. If the card you've picked doesn't fit my rule, I will say "no," and you can put it outside the yarn circle. Each person can only pick one card at each turn. Once you've found a couple of cards that fit the rule you can try to reason out what my rule is, but you can only try to guess my rule when it is your turn to pick a card.

(The teacher takes one group and plays one simple round with the teacher as a rule card holder. The other students gather round to watch.)

As you can see this is a game that requires reasoning and some very careful thinking. Many of the things you will be doing at learning stations will require reasoning and thinking. When people have such a difficult problem to solve, one thing they can do is *find out what others think.*

We are going to practice finding out what others think. When it is your turn and you have an idea what the rule is, ask the two other players in your group what they think about your idea. You might say, "I think the rule is all blue shapes. Do you think that's the rule?" If they say yes or no, ask them *to tell why* they think that. After you listen to what they say or if they don't know, ask the other person the same questions. Then *make up your own mind* about what you think is the rule and ask the rule card holder.

Discussion

Have the students practice asking each other what they think and why they think so. Discuss with them why it is important to try and tell why. This is an important new skill.

A third rule is also important preparation for working at learning stations. Because each student is responsible for his or her own report, it is important that all the students feel responsible for making their own decisions about what to do after consulting others.

All these new behaviors ("Find out what others think," "Tell why," and "Make your own decision") should be printed on a chart and prominently displayed.

As in the previous skillbuilder there should be an observer. The two behaviors an observer can hear and see are

> Finding out what others think.
> Telling why.

The person who is the observer should have a simple check sheet parallel to the one for Master Designer, but with the new behaviors on it.

You are now ready to have each group play the game and take turns with the various roles. One person is the rule card holder, one is the observer, and the other three are players. After each round, other group members get to be rule card holder and observer. The new rule card holder picks up a new card from the deck, which is face down.

After the game, have the observers report how many times they saw the new behaviors on the round they scored. Ask the students to discuss whether or not it was helpful to them to get other people's opinions. See if you can pick up some good examples of student's telling "why" if they don't come up with these themselves. Have them comment on what it is like to hear opinions different from one's own and to have to consider those ideas before making up one's own mind. Ask them if they know of any other situation that is like this. Point out that they will have to do this at the learning stations.

RAINBOW LOGIC*

This is an exercise developed by the Family Math program to give the students practice in communicating their deductive thinking and spatial reasoning. Students must deduce through a series of questions

---

*Adapted from Stenmark, Thompson, & Cossey, *Family Math*, Lawrence Hall of Science, Copyright 1987 Regents University of California. All rights reserved.

the pattern of a 3 × 3 color grid. The grid is constructed using rules about the permissible ways in which squares may be placed. Within those rules the group must discuss and decide on the best questions to ask of the grid designer.

Materials
Colored paper squares for each player
4 each of each of 4 colors (more than needed for solution)
3 × 3 grids

Procedure
For the first round, the teacher may be the grid designer. A group can be selected to demonstrate the exercise and the rest of the class can gather round to watch. After the first round, students should take turns being the grid designer in their separate groups. Group sizes can vary from 3 to 5. The person who is the grid designer can also play the role of observer.

The grid designer prepares a secret 3 × 3 color grid, using 3 squares of each color.

> *Rule*: All of the squares of the same color must be connected by at least one full side. See Figure A.6 for examples of permissible and impermissible grids.

The goal is for the players to be able to give the location of all colors on the grid after as few questions as possible. Therefore the group should *discuss and decide* before asking the gridkeeper a question. In the course of the discussion students should share the logic of their thinking. Why will this question get the maximum amount of useful information for solving the problem? During this discussion, there are two new behaviors that the students should learn:

> Discuss and decide.
> Give reasons for your suggestions.

Rules for asking and answering questions:

> Players ask for the colors in a particular row or column (rows are horizontal, columns are vertical).
> The grid designer gives the colors, *but not necessarily in order.*
> Each player should use a grid and colored paper squares to keep track of clues.
> Squares may be put *beside* the row or column until exact places are determined.

FIGURE A.6: Grids for "Rainbow Logic"

Example of a Secret Grid

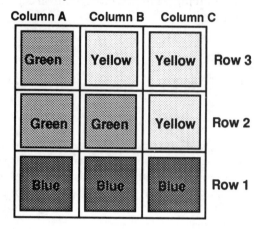

Patterns Like the Ones Below are Not Allowed

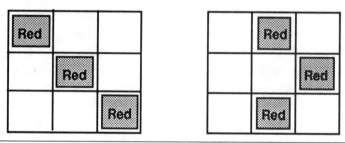

Note: If this seems too easy for the class, try playing with a 4 × 4 grid with the same rules.

Discussion

The observer for a particular round should keep track of how often people give reasons for their suggestions. The observer should also watch the character of the discussion to see if people really discussed before they came to a decision. Perhaps one person jumped in and asked the question of the grid designer before everyone in the group was heard from or before a controversy was actually resolved.

After most groups have had the chance to complete a few rounds of the exercise, the teacher should stop the action and have observers from each group report what they have seen. Then the class may discuss how to improve the process of discussion and the process of giving reasons. Let the class proceed to give everyone else a turn at being grid designer and observer. After they have finished the final round, ask the observers to come up and form a panel to discuss whether what they heard improved discussion and giving of reasons in the group in the second part of the lesson. Alternatively, students could write about what they have learned concerning the three cooperative norms and how they fit into groupwork in their subject matter.

Preparing Students for Groupwork That Features Group Discussion

EPSTEIN'S FOUR-STAGE ROCKET

This is the original task designed by Epstein (1972) to improve discussion skills of any age group. There are some minor adaptations of the original version in the material presented.

Pretest
Explain to the class that in order to prepare for the groupwork they need to learn what it takes to have a good group discussion. Divide the class into five-person groups. Give the groups a highly interesting task to discuss. (Two sample discussion tasks are given at the end of Appendix A.) The teacher circulates, listening, observing, and taking notes on examples of good and bad discussion technique. The groups are allowed to discuss for five minutes.

Practicing the four stages
After the pretest, hold a group discussion on what makes for good discussion and what the barriers are. Tell the class that they are going to practice four skills that are necessary so that a discussion can take off like a rocket (use an illustration of a rocket with four stages) by following the instructions given below.

Stage I, Conciseness—"getting quickly to the point and not beating around the bush."
Select a timekeeper who will watch the clock and keep time for the group. Keep on discussing the subject for five minutes. The timekeeper makes sure that *each person talks for only fifteen seconds.*
Stage II, Listening—"paying attention to what is being said."
Select a new timekeeper. Keep on discussing the same subject for

five more minutes, again making sure that each person talks for only fifteen seconds. This time, however, *each person must wait three seconds after the person before has spoken before he or she may speak.*

Stage III, Reflecting—"repeating out loud to the group something of what the person before you has said."

Select a new timekeeper. Keep on discussing the same subject, making sure that each person talks for only fifteen seconds and that he or she waits three seconds after the person before has spoken before he or she speaks. In addition, *everyone who speaks must begin by repeating to the group something that was said by the person who spoke immediately before.* This is called *reflecting.* The person who had spoken before has to nod his or her head to mean yes if he or she thinks this reflection is right. The new speaker may not continue until he or she correctly reflects what the person before has said.

Stage IV, Everyone contributes—"all the people in the group have to speak"

Select a new timekeeper. Keep on discussing the same subject for five more minutes. All previous rules apply, as well as a new one. *No one may speak a second time until everyone in the group has spoken.*

After each stage ask each timekeeper to report on how well their group did on the skill being practiced. The timekeeper may have other observations to make about how difficult it was and what happened. Remind the class why each skill is important.

Posttest

Select a person as observer who has not yet had a chance to play a role like timekeeper. Hold five more minutes of discussion without having to observe the rules but trying to use the skills of *conciseness, listening, reflecting,* and *contributions by everyone.* Observers will note down every time they see good examples of each of these behaviors. You may want to create a scoring sheet.

After the posttest, ask observers to tell what they observed. Also ask the whole class what were some of the differences between the pretest and the posttest.

Note: Unless the class has had some previous experience with discussion, you will find that they will finish discussion tasks very rapidly. You will need to have alternative questions or tasks prepared. Sample discussion tasks are given at the end of this Appendix.

IMPROVING GROUP PROCESS SKILLS

The Four-Stage Rocket may be enough to get the groupwork started. However, there are additional skills, especially for group projects, that become more important as groups attempt longer-term, more ambitious projects. One can develop lists of constructive and destructive behaviors for improving group process skills.

Constructive behaviors are ways that help to get the group's work done. A skillful group member

Has *new ideas*
Requests or provides information
Explains ideas
Puts ideas together
Asks if everyone is ready to decide what to do.

Especially *constructive behaviors* are those that assist with the smooth operation of the group. A constructive group member

Asks quiet group members what they think
Listens with interest to what other people say
Praises good ideas and suggestions
Is willing to compromise.

Destructive behaviors are common problems that arise in groups and often result in hurt feelings and a poor group product. A destructive group member

Talks too much
Listens very little
Insists on having his or her ideas accepted
Fails to do something about the destructive behavior of others
Criticizes people rather than their ideas
Lets other people do all the work.

Choose a small number of these behaviors that you think are of critical importance based on what you think the group will need or problems that you have observed during discussions. It is always better if the class members can select behaviors that need work on the basis of their own experience. Explain to the class that this exercise will help them with these prticular skills.

Divide the class into discussion groups after you have presented to them the set of behaviors they are going to be working on. Always use the same label to refer to the selected behaviors. Select one observer for each group who will write down every time one of these particular behaviors occurs. Draw up a scoring sheet. Take observers aside in advance and make sure they know how to observe these particular behaviors. Give the groups a discussion topic that they can work on for five or ten minutes.

Stop the discussion and ask observers to report what they have seen and scored. Pull out from the discussion some good strategies that have been used or alternative strategies to deal with problems that have arisen. The same basic format can be used for any number of skills that you think require practice.

Sample Discussion Tasks

SPACE SHIP

The object of this game is to select seven persons to go into a space ship for a voyage to a new planet. You have just been alerted that a giant meteor is on collision course with the planet earth and will smash into the general area of the United States. Therefore, it is very likely the end of human civilization as we know it. The space ship has the capacity to set up life on a new planet. Eleven persons have been chosen by lot to go on the ship; however, an error was made, and now it turns out that there is only room for seven. Your group must decide which seven persons will go to start life on the new planet. Remember, only seven persons can fit in the ship. You must have an agreement of the entire group before a selection can be made.

1. A 30-year-old male symphony orchestra violin player.
2. A 67-year-old male minister
3. A 23-year-old engineer and his 21-year-old wife (they refuse to be separated)
4. A 40-year-old policeman who refuses to be separated from his gun
5. A male student of your own age from your school
6. A 35-year-old male high school dropout, recently arrested for armed robbery
7. A 32-year-old female sixth-grade teacher
8. A 40-year-old female doctor (medical)
9. A 50-year-old female artist and sculptor
10. A 25-year-old male poet
11. A 1-year-old female child

ALLIGATOR RIVER

Once there was a girl named Abigail who was in love with a boy named Gregory. Gregory had an unfortunate accident and broke his glasses. Abigail, being a true friend, volunteered to take them to be repaired. But the repair shop was across the river, and during a flash flood the bridge was washed away. Poor Gregory could see nothing without his glasses, so Abigail was desperate to get across the river to the repair shop. While she was standing forlornly on the bank of the river, clutching the broken glasses in her hand, a boy named Sinbad glided by in a rowboat.

She asked Sinbad if he would take her across. He agreed on the condition what while she was having the glasses repaired, she would go to a nearby store and steal a transistor radio that he had been wanting. Abigail refused to do this and went to see a friend named Ivan who had a boat.

When Abigail told Ivan her problem, he said he was too busy to help her out and didn't want to become involved. Abigail, feeling that she had no other choice, returned to Sinbad and told him she would agree to his plan.

When Abigail returned the repaired glasses to Gregory, she told him what she had had to do. Gregory was so mad at what she had done he told her that he never wanted to see her again.

Abigail, upset, turned to Slug with her tale of woe. Slug was so sorry for Abigail that he promised her he would get even with Gregory. They went to the school playground where Gregory was playing ball and Abigail watched happily while Slug beat Gregory up and broke his new glasses.

Rank these characters from "best" to "worst": Abigail, Gregory, Sinbad, Ivan, Slug. *Give reasons for your decisions.* (Simon, Howe, & Kirschenbaum, 1972, pp. 292–293)

Conflict Resolution Strategies for Groupwork*

Students are first introduced to two new tools for conflict resolution: "I feel" statements, and positive requests. The teacher introduces the new ways of talking, providing definitions, examples, and opportunities to practice. These statements are contrasted with blaming statements; the students learn that these are substitutes for the more familiar strategy of blaming others. This discussion with the whole class is followed by a communication worksheet on which students practice translating blaming statements into "I feel" statements and positive requests.

---

*The materials in this section were developed by Diane Kepner.

TEACHER-LED DISCUSSION AND STUDENT PRACTICE

"I feel" statements

Most of the time when students feel hurt and become angry because of something someone else has done, they confront each other with accusations in ways that only escalate conflict. "I Feel" statements provide a constructive way of expressing unpleasant feelings to others. They enable us to take responsibility for our feelings and the way we react to what others say and do. At the same time these statements let others know how their behavior affects us—without blame.

Blaming statements usually begin with "You" and focus on the other person in a highly judgmental and negative way. "I feel" statements focus on our own feelings in response to the other person's behavior. They consist of three parts: identifying the behavior, expressing the feelings experienced as a result of the behavior, and explaining the reasons for those feelings. A useful formula for phrasing "I feel" statements is:

> When you . . . (State problem behavior)
> I feel . . . (Express feeling)
> Because . . . (State reasons for your feeling)

Student Practice.   Share with the class the following examples of "You" statements and contrast them with "I Feel" statements related to the same topic. The examples are all taken from common conflicts in small groups. Have a small group of students come up and act out the two alternative responses. Have the class analyze the "I feel" statements in terms of the formula. Can they construct alternative "I feel" statements that fit the formula? You can use buzz groups for this exercise.

Situation #1: A member of your group interrupts you constantly when you are talking.

> "You" statement: "You're so rude! You never let me say anything!"
> "I feel" statement: "When you interrupt me, I feel really hurt because I think that what I have to say is important too."

Situation #2: Two members of the group are holding the task cards so that you can't see the diagrams.

> "You" statement: "You guys are always hogging everything!"
> "I feel" statement: "I feel left out when you guys have the cards between you because I can't follow what's going on."

Situation #3: A member of your group is busy shooting paper wads at someone in another group and talking to members of the other group.

"You" statement: "You're such a goof-off. You never help."
"I feel" statement: "When you start doing things with people in other groups I feel really upset because we need everyone's help to get this project done on time."

Positive requests

Most problems are not solved just because an "I feel" statement has been made. Group members must listen carefully to what has been said. For the group to respond constructively, members need to know what should be done. Positive requests can help the group move from understanding feelings to action. This requires that we focus not on what we don't want the other person to do, but on what specific actions we do want the other person to take. We have to ask ourselves "What do I need to have you do differently and what will that new action look like?" It requires being specific and positive rather than vague and negative in our requests of others.

Student Practice. Go over the following examples with the class. Ask them to describe why the third statement is specific and how it contrasts with the second statement. Positive requests usually begin with "I want you to," "I would," "I'd like you to," and "I need you to." Students may resist the formality of the language in these and the "I feel" statements. After some initial practice in following the formula, you may want to let them put their responses into their "own language" but be sure that you follow this up with an examination and discussion of whether or not their own terms change the nature of the message and, if so, how.

1. Negative: "Stop interrupting me."
   Vague: "I want you to listen to me."
   Positive and specific: "I want you to wait until I'm finished before you start talking."
2. Negative: "Stop hogging all the cards!"
   Vague: "I want you to share the cards with me."
   Positive and specific: "I need you to put the cards in the middle of the table so I can see."
3. Negative: "I want you to stop messing around."
   Vague: "I want you to help our group."
   Positive and specific: "I would like you to fill in the chart with the information from our notes."

Putting the "I feel" statement and the positive requests together creates a powerful tool for communication by helping students to express their feelings and request changes in others in a direct and honest way. Go back through the examples under "I feel" statements and have the class create positive action statements for these examples.

COMMUNICATION WORKSHEET

As you work in your groups problems will occur with other members. Use your new knowledge to let them know how you feel and what you need from them. Practice using "I feel" statements and positive requests to express yourself and avoid using blaming messages that add to the problem.

For each of the situations below, write a blaming message followed by an "I feel" statement and a positive request.

Then try writing some situations of your own based on real group experiences that you've had or observed.

1. One member in your group is doing all the building on the project. Every time you try to make a suggestion you are ignored. When you pick something up to try to help, it is taken away from you.
2. One member of your group has been wandering around visiting friends while the rest of you worked on the poster for your presentation. Now just as you are about to finish he/she bumps into your desk causing you to make an ugly mark all the way across the page.
3. There are only three people in your group. The other two are good friends but you don't know them very well. They are sitting close together and acting as if you don't even exist.
4. All the other members in your group are actively discussing the questions for your activity. You would like to say something too but every time they ask you for your opinion, they move on to someone else before you've had a chance to put your thoughts into words.
5. One member of your group always gets good grades on all of his/her regular class work but in the group he/she never contributes. You suspect that he/she knows the way to solve the problem you're all working on.

APPENDIX B

Tools for Groupwork Evaluation

SAMPLE STUDENT QUESTIONNAIRE

Name: _____

Please mark with an "X" on the line to the left of each answer that is most like how you feel for each question. Remember, this is not a test. There are no right answers. I want to know what you think.

Section A

1. How interesting did you find your work in the group?
    _____ a. Very interesting.
    _____ b. Fairly interesting.
    _____ c. Somewhat interesting.
    _____ d. Not very interesting.
    _____ e. I was not interested at all.
2. How difficult did you find your work in the group?
    _____ a. Extremely difficult.
    _____ b. Fairly difficult.
    _____ c. Sometimes difficult.
    _____ d. Not too difficult—just about right.
    _____ e. Very easy.
3. Did you understand exactly what the group was supposed to do?
    _____ a. I knew just what to do.
    _____ b. At first I didn't understand.
    _____ c. It was never clear to me.
4. *For Multiple Ability Tasks*
    a. What abilities did you think were important for doing a good job on this task?

   b. Was there one ability on which you thought you did very well?
   _____ Yes   _____ No
5. How many times did you have the chance to talk during the group
   session today?
   _____ a. None.
   _____ b. One or two times.
   _____ c. Three to four times.
   _____ d. Five or more times.
6. If you talked less than you wanted to, what were the main reasons?
   _____ a. I felt afraid to give my opinion.
   _____ b. Somebody else interrupted me.
   _____ c. I was not given the chance to give my opinion.
   _____ d. I talked as much as I wanted to.
   _____ e. Nobody paid attention to what I said.
   _____ f. I was not interested in the problem.
   _____ g. I was not feeling well today.
7. Did you get along with everybody in your group?
   _____ a. With few of them.
   _____ b. With half of them.
   _____ c. With most of them.
   _____ d. With all of them.
   _____ e. With none of them.
8. How many students listened to each other's ideas?
   _____ a. Only a few of them.
   _____ b. Half of them.
   _____ c. Most of them.
   _____ d. All of them, except one.
   _____ e. All of them.

Section B

1. Who did the most talking in your group today?
2. Who did the least talking in your group today?
3. Who had the best ideas in your group today?
4. Who did the most to direct the discussion?
5. Would you like to work with this group again?
   _____ Yes   _____ No
   If not, why not?
6. How well do you think the facilitator did today in his or her job?

GUIDE TO ANALYZING THE STUDENT QUESTIONNAIRE

I. What percentage of the class found the task uninteresting, too difficult, or confusing? (Questions A, B, and C below will show you how to calculate the answer using student responses to Section A, questions 1–3.)

    A. What percentage of the students reported the work was not very interesting or that they were not interested at all? (Add up the number of students who chose d or e on question 1. Divide this number by total who turned in questionnaires to obtain a percentage.)

    B. What percentage of the students reported that the work was extremely difficult or very easy? (Add up the number of students who chose a or e on question 2. Use the same procedure as above to obtain a percentage.)

    C. What percentage of the students reported that the instructions were never clear to them? (Determine the number of students who chose c in question 3. Follow the same procedure as above to obtain a percentage.)

II. *For multiple ability tasks:* Did the students see the task as involving multiple abilities? (Use Section A, question 4.)

    A. How many students were able to list more than one ability? (Question 4a)

    B. How many students were able to list one ability on which they thought they did well? (Question 4b)

    C. How many of the abilities listed were like those in ordinary schoolwork? (Question 4b)

III. How was the group process? Are there special problems that need further work?

    A. What kinds of problems are checked off frequently on Section A, question 6?

    B. How many students report getting along with half or fewer members of their group? (Section A, question 7; add up a, b, and e.)

    C. How many students report that half or fewer members of their group listened? (Section A, question 8; add up a and b.)

IV. How did the low status students feel about their experience? (Pull out their questionnaires and make tabulations listed below.)

A. How many of these students found the task uninteresting, too difficult, or confusing? How does this number compare to the total number of students in the class who felt that way? *If a much higher percentage of low status students were unhappy with the task than the overall percentage for the class calculated in questions 1–3, then your task was particularly unsuccessful with low status students.*

B. *For Multiple Ability Tasks:* How many of the low status students reported that there was an ability on which they thought they did well? (Section A, question 4b.) *If the multiple ability treatment is successful, practically all these students should answer yes.*

C. Were these students more likely to report that they rarely participated than the rest of the class? (Count up how many of the low status students chose a or b on question 5 in Section A. Now do the same for the rest of the class.) *If more than half of the low status students reported poor participation, while only 25 percent or fewer of the students in the rest of the class said they participated rarely, then you still have a status problem in participation.*

D. Were there some particular low status students for whom this experience was not a good one? Take those low status students who report little participation on question 5 and examine their questionnaire as a whole to see if you can find out what the source of the trouble was.

V. How successful was each group in achieving equal status and good group process? (Rearrange the questionnaires so you have all the ones from each group together.)

A. Did some groups report more interpersonal problems than others? Or were complaints pretty well spread across groups? (Section A, questions 6, 7, and 8.) If three or more members of the same group make one of these complaints about their experience, one could reasonably infer that this particular group had interpersonal difficulty.

B. Were there any groups in which the low status student was chosen by at least two others as having had the best ideas? (Section B, question 3.) This would indicate that you have been successful in treating the status problem in at least some of your groups.

C. In how many groups did almost everyone choose one of the low status students as having done the least talking? (Section B, question 2.) This is a group where you have not achieved equal status behavior. Check the group's questionnaires over carefully. You may want to appoint this student as facilitator next time.

    D. How were the evaluations of the facilitator in each group? (Section B, question 6.)

    E. If the low status student was a facilitator, was he or she chosen by at least some group members as having done the most to direct the discussion? (Section B, question 4.)

VI. How good were the relations between students of different racial or ethnic or language groups? (Divide the questionnaires by racial, ethnic, or linguistic group membership.)

    A. Did most of the minority students report getting along with most or all of the other students in their group? (Section A, question 7.)

    B. What proportion of minority vs. majority group said that they would not like to work with their group again? (Section B, question 5.) Ideally, the proportion should not be much above 15 percent in either category, and it is certainly not a good sign if the proportion is much higher among minorities than among majority students.

References

Aaronson, E. (1978). *The jigsaw classroom.* Beverly Hills, CA: Sage.

Ahmadjian, J. (1980). *Academic status and reading achievement: Modifying the effects of the self-fulfilling prophecy.* Unpublished doctoral dissertation, Stanford University, Stanford, CA.

American Association for the Advancement of Science. (1989). *Science for all Americans.* Washington, DC: Author.

Anderson, L. M. (1982). *Student response to seatwork: Implications for the study of students' cognitive processing.* Research Series No. 102. East Lansing: Michigan State University, Institute for Research on Teaching.

Awang Had, B. S. (1972). *Effects of status and task outcome structures upon observable power and prestige order of small task-oriented groups.* Unpublished doctoral dissertation, Stanford University, Stanford, CA.

Bandura, A. (1969). *Principles of behavior modification.* New York: Holt, Rinehart & Winston.

Bassarear, T., & Davidson, N. (1992). The use of small group learning situations in mathematics instruction as a tool to develop thinking. In N. Davidson & T. Worsham (Eds.), *Enhancing thinking through cooperative learning* (pp. 236–250). New York: Teachers College Press.

Bavelas, A. (1973). The five squares problem—An instructional aid in group cooperation. *Studies in Personnel Psychology, 5,* 29–38.

Berger, J., Conner, T., & McKeown, W. (1974). Evaluations and the formation and maintenance of performance expectations. In J. Berger, T. Conner, & H. Fisek (Eds.), *Expectation states theory: A theoretical research program* (pp. 27–51). Cambridge, MA: Winthrop.

Berger, J., Rosenholtz, S. J., & Zelditch, M., Jr. (1980). Status organizing processes. *Annual Review of Sociology, 6,* 479–508.

Berliner, D., Fisher, C., Filby, N., Marliave, R., Cahen, L., Dishaw, M., & Moore, J. (1978). *Beginning teacher evaluation study—Teaching behaviors, academic learning time and student achievement. Final report of phase II-B.* San Francisco: Far West Laboratory.

Bower, A. (1990). *The effect of a multiple ability treatment on status and learning in the cooperative social studies classroom.* Unpublished doctoral dissertation, Stanford University, Stanford, CA.

Brinton, D. M., Snow, M. A., & Wesche, M. B. (1990). *Content-based second language instruction.* Boston: Heinle & Heinle.

Cazden, C. (1988). *Classroom discourse: The language of teaching.* Portsmouth, NH: Heinemann.

Cohen, E. G. (1972). Interracial interaction disability. *Human Relations, 25,* 9–24.

Cohen, E. G. (1982). Expectations states and interracial interaction in school settings. *Annual Review of Sociology, 8,* 209–235.

Cohen, E. G. (1984). Talking and working together: Status, interaction and learning. In P. Peterson, L. C. Wilkinson, & M. Hallinan (Eds.), *The social context of instruction: Group organization and group processes* (pp. 171–187). New York: Academic Press.

Cohen, E. G. (1988, July). *Producing equal status behavior in cooperative learning.* Paper presented at the convention of the International Association for the Study of Cooperation in Education, Shefayim, Israel.

Cohen, E. G. (1991). Teaching in multiculturally heterogeneous classrooms: Findings from a model program. *McGill Journal of Education, 26,* 7–23.

Cohen, E. G. (1992). *Restructuring the classroom: Conditions for productive small groups.* Madison, WI: Center on the Organization and Restructuring of Schools, University of Wisconsin–Madison.

Cohen, E. G., & Chatfield, M. (1991). *Complex instruction in the middle school: Implementation manual.* Stanford, CA: Stanford University, Program for Complex Instruction.

Cohen, E. G., & Intili, J. K. (1982). *Interdependence and management in bilingual classrooms: Final report II.* (NIE Contract #NIE-G-80-0217). Stanford, CA: Stanford University, Center for Educational Research.

Cohen, E. G., Lockheed, M., & Lohman, M. (1976). Center for interracial co-operation: A field experiment. *Sociology of Education, 49,* 47–58.

Cohen, E. G., Lotan, R., & Catanzarite, L. (1990). Treating status problems in the cooperative classroom. In S. Sharan (Ed.), *Cooperative learning: Theory and research* (pp. 203–229). New York: Praeger.

Cohen, E. G., Lotan, R., & Leechor, C. (1989). Can classrooms learn? *Sociology of Education, 62,* 75–94.

Cohen, E. G., & Roper, S. (1972). Modification of interracial interaction disability: An application of status characteristic theory. *American Sociological Review, 37,* 648–655.

Cohen, E. G., & Sharan, S. (1980). Modifying status relations in Israeli youth. *Journal of Cross-Cultural Psychology, 11,* 364–384.

Comprehensive Test of Basic Skills (CTBS). (1981). Monterey, CA: McGraw Hill.

Cook, T. (1974). *Producing equal status interaction between Indian and white boys in British Columbia.* Unpublished doctoral dissertation, Stanford University, Stanford, CA.

Cummins, J. (1979). Linguistic interdependence and the educational development of bilingual children. *Review of Educational Research, 49,* 222–251.

Dar, Y., & Resh, N. (1986). Classroom intellectual composition and academic achievement. *American Educational Research Journal, 23,* 357–374.

Davidson, N. (1985). Small group learning and teaching in mathematics: A selective review of the research. In R. Slavin, S. Sharan, S. Kagan, R. Hertz-Lazarowitz, G. Webb, & R. Schmuck (Eds.), *Learning to cooperate, Cooperating to learn* (pp. 211–230). New York: Plenum.

De Avila, E. A. (1981). *Multicultural improvement of cognitive abilities: Final report to State of California, Department of Education.* Stanford, CA: Stanford University, School of Education.

De Avila, E. A., & Duncan, S. E. (1977). *Language assessment scales, level I* (2nd ed.). Corte Madera, CA: Linguametrics Group.

De Avila, E. A., & Duncan, S. E. (1980). *Finding Out/Descubrimiento.* Corte Madera, CA: Linguametrics Group.

Dembo, M., & McAuliffe, T. (1987). Effects of perceived ability and grade status on social interaction and influence in cooperative groups. *Journal of Educational Psychology, 79,* 415–423.

Deutsch, M. (1968). The effects of cooperation and competition upon group process. In D. Cartwright & A. Zander (Eds.), *Group dynamics* (pp. 319–353). New York: Harper & Row.

Durling, R., & Shick, C. (1976). Concept attainment by pairs and individuals as a function of vocalization. *Journal of Educational Psychology, 68,* 83–91.

Egan, K., & Marsing, D. (1984). *Teaching the whip kick using a multiability group.* Unpublished manuscript, Stanford University, Stanford, CA.

Ehrlich, D. E. (1991). *Moving beyond cooperation: Developing science thinking in interdependent groups.* Unpublished doctoral dissertation, Stanford University, Stanford, CA.

Epstein, C. (1972). *Affective subjects in the classroom: Exploring race, sex and drugs.* Scranton, PA: Intext Educational Publications.

Faltis, C. J., & Merino, B. J. (1992). Toward a definition of exemplary teachers in bilingual multicultural school settings. In R. V. Padilla & A. H. Benavides (Eds.), *Critical perspectives on bilingual education research* (pp. 276–299). Tempe, AZ: Bilingual Press.

Gardner, H. (1983). *Frames of mind: The theory of multiple intelligences.* New York: Basic Books.

Gould, S. J. (1981). *The mismeasure of man.* New York: Norton.

Graves, N., & Graves, T. (1991). Candida Graves: Complex teamwork in action. *Cooperative Learning, 12,* 14–16.

Graves, T., & Graves, N. (1985). Broken Circles (game). Santa Cruz, CA.

Hall, J. (1971). Decisions, decisions, decisions. *Psychology Today, 5,* 51.

Hoffman, D., & Cohen, E. G. (1972, April). *An exploratory study to determine the effects of generalized performance expectations upon activity and influence of students engaged in a group simulation game.* Paper presented at American Educational Research Association, Chicago.

Huber, G., & Eppler, R. (1990). Team learning in German classrooms: processes and outcomes. In S. Sharan (Ed.), *Cooperative learning: Theory and research* (pp. 151–171). New York: Praeger.

Intili, J. K. (1977). *Structural conditions in the school that facilitate reflective decision-making.* Unpublished doctoral dissertation, Stanford University, Stanford, CA.

Johnson, D., & Johnson, R. (1985). Classroom conflict: Controversy versus debate in learning groups. *American Educational Research Journal, 22,* 237–256.

Johnson, D., & Johnson, R. (1990). Cooperative learning and achievement. In

S. Sharan (Ed.), *Cooperative learning: Theory and research* (pp. 23–37). New York: Praeger.

Johnson, D., & Johnson, R. (1992). Encouraging thinking through constructive controversy. In N. Davidson & T. Worsham (Eds.), *Enhancing thinking through cooperative learning* (pp. 120–137). New York: Teachers College Press.

Johnson, D., Johnson, R., & Maruyama, G. (1983). Interdependence and interpersonal attraction among heterogeneous and homogeneous individuals: A theoretical formulation and a meta-analysis of the research. *Review of Educational Research, 53,* 5–54.

Johnson, D., Johnson, R., & Maruyama, G. (1984). Goal interdependence and interpersonal attraction in heterogeneous classrooms: A metanalysis. In N. Miller & M. Brewer (Eds.), *Groups in contact: The psychology of desegregation* (pp. 187–212). Orlando, FL: Academic Press.

Johnson, D. W., Maruyama, G., Johnson, R., Nelson, D., & Skon, L. (1981). Effects of cooperative, competitive and individualistic goal structure on achievement: A meta-analysis. *Psychological Bulletin, 89,* 47–62.

Kerckhoff, A. C. (1986). Effects of ability grouping in British secondary schools. *American Sociological Review, 51,* 842–858.

Kinney, K., & Leonard, M. (1984). *Groupwork lessons: Geometry.* Unpublished manuscript, Stanford University, Stanford, CA.

Krashen, S. D. (1988). Bilingual education and second language acquisition theory. In California State Department of Education, *Schooling and language minority students: A theoretical framework* (pp. 51–79). Los Angeles: Evaluation, Dissemination and Assessment Center, California State University.

Kreidler, J. (1984). *Creative conflict resolution.* Glenview, IL: Scott Foresman & Co.

Leal, A. (1985). *Sex inequities in classroom interaction: An evaluation of an intervention.* Unpublished doctoral dissertation, Stanford University, Stanford, CA.

Leechor, C. (1988). *How high achieving and low achieving students differentially benefit from working together in cooperative small groups.* Unpublished doctoral dissertation. Stanford University, Stanford, CA.

Lindholm, K. J., & Aclan, Z. (1991). Bilingual proficiency as a bridge to academic achievement: Results from bilingual/immersion programs. *Journal of Education, 173,* 99–113.

Lockheed, M. S., Harris, A. M., & Nemceff, W. P. (1983). Sex and social influence: Does sex function as a status characteristic in mixed-sex groups? *Journal of Educational Psychology, 75,* 877–888.

Marquis, A., & Cooper, C. (1982, July). *Peer interaction and learning in cooperative settings.* Paper presented at the Second International Conference on Cooperation in Education, Provo, UT.

McGroarty, M. (1989). The benefits of cooperative learning arrangements in second language instruction. *National Association for Bilingual Association Journal, 13*(2), 127–143.

McLaughlin, B. (1985). *Second-language acquisition in childhood. Volume 2: School-age children.* Hillsdale, NJ: Lawrence Erlbaum.

Miller, N., Brewer, M., & Edwards, K. (1985). Cooperative interaction in de-segregated settings: A laboratory analogue. *Journal of Social Issues, 41,* 63–79.

Miller, N., & Harrington, H. J. (1990). A situational identity perspective on cultural diversity and teamwork in the classroom. In S. Sharan (Ed.), *Cooperative learning: Theory and research* (pp. 39–75). New York: Praeger.

Morris, R. (1977). *A normative intervention to equalize participation in task-oriented groups.* Unpublished doctoral dissertation, Stanford University, Stanford, CA.

Murray, F. (1972). Acquisition of conservation through social interaction. *Developmental Psychology, 6,* 1–6.

National Commission on Social Studies in the Schools. (1989). *Charting a course: Social studies for the 21st century.* Washington, DC: Author.

National Council of Teachers of Mathematics. (1989). *Curriculum and evaluation standards for school mathematics.* Reston, VA: Author.

Navarrete, C. (1980). *Finding Out/Descubrimiento: A developmental approach to language and culture in a bilingual elementary classroom.* Unpublished manuscript, Stanford University, Stanford, CA.

Navarrete, C. (1985). *Problem resolution in small group interaction: A bilingual classroom study.* Unpublished doctoral dissertation, Stanford University, Stanford, CA.

Neves, A. (1983). *The effect of various input on the second language acquisition of Mexican-American children in nine elementary school classrooms.* Unpublished doctoral dissertation, Stanford University, Stanford, CA.

Newmann, F., & Thompson, J. A. (1987). *Effects of cooperative learning on achievement in secondary schools: A summary of research.* Madison: National Center on Effective Secondary Schools, University of Wisconsin–Madison.

Nystrand, M., Gamoran, A., & Heck, M. J. (1991). *Small groups in English: When do they help students and how are they best used?* Madison: Center on the Organization and Restructuring of Schools, The University of Wisconsin–Madison.

Perrow, C. B. (1961). A framework for the comparative analysis of organizations. *American Sociological Review, 32,* 194–208.

Pfeiffer, J., & Jones, F. E. (1970). *A handbook of structural experiences for human relations training* (Vol. 1). Iowa City: University Associated Press.

Robbins, A. (1977). *Fostering equal-status interaction through the establishment of consistent staff behaviors and appropriate situational norms.* Unpublished doctoral dissertation, Stanford University, Stanford, CA.

Rosenberg, M. B. (1983). *A model for nonviolent communication.* Baltimore, MD: New Society Publishers.

Rosenholtz, S. J. (1977). *The multiple ability curriculum: An intervention against the self-fulfilling prophecy.* Unpublished dissertation, Stanford University, Stanford, CA.

Rosenholtz, S. J. (1985). Modifying status expectations in the traditional classroom. In J. Berger & M. Zelditch, Jr. (Eds.), *Status, rewards, and influence* (pp. 445–470). San Francisco: Jossey Bass.

Rosenholtz, S. J., & Cohen, E. G. (1985). Activating ethnic status. In J. Berger & M. Zelditch, Jr. (Eds.), *Status, rewards, and influence* (pp. 430–444). San Francisco: Jossey Bass.

Rosenholtz, S. J., & Wilson, B. (1980). The effects of classroom structure on shared perceptions of ability. *American Educational Research Journal, 17,* 175–182.

Schwartz, D. L., Black, J. B., & Strange, J. (1991, April). *Dyads have a fourfold advantage over individuals inducing abstract rules.* Paper presented at annual meeting of the American Educational Research Association, Chicago.

Sharan, S., & Hertz-Lazarowitz, R. (1980). A group investigation method of cooperative learning in the classroom. In S. Sharan, A. P. Hare, C. Webb, & R. Hertz-Lazarowitz (Eds.), *Contributions to the study of cooperation in education* (pp. 19–46). Provo, UT: Brigham Young University Press.

Sharan, S., Hertz-Lazarowitz, R., & Ackerman, Z. (1980). Academic achievement of elementary school children in small group versus whole-class instruction. *Journal of Experimental Education, 48,* 125–129.

Sharan, S., Kussell, P., Hertz-Lazarowitz, R., Begarano, Y., Raviv, S., & Sharan, Y. (1984). *Cooperative learning in the classroom: Research in desegregated schools.* Hillsdale, NJ: Lawrence Erlbaum.

Sharan, S., & Shachar, H. (1988). *Language and learning in the cooperative classroom.* New York: Spring-Verlag.

Sharan, S., & Sharan, Y. (1976). *Small-group teaching.* Englewood Cliffs, NJ: Educational Technology Publications.

Sharan, Y., & Sharan, S. (1992). *Expanding cooperative learning through group investigation.* New York: Teachers College Press.

Simon, S., Howe, L. W., & Kirchenbaum, H. (1972). Values clarification. New York: Hart Publishing.

Slavin, R. E. (1983). *Cooperative learning.* New York: Longmann.

Slavin, R. E. (1987). Ability grouping and student achievement in elementary schools: A best-evidence synthesis. *Review of Educational Research, 57,* 293–336.

Smith, K., Johnson, D. W., & Johnson, R. T. (1981). Can conflict be constructive? Controversy versus concurrence seeking in learning groups. *Journal of Educational Psychology, 73,* 651–663.

Solomon, R. D., Davidson, N., & Solomon, E. C. L. (1992). Some thinking skills and social skills that facilitate cooperative learning. In N. Davidson & T. Worsham (Eds.), *Enhancing thinking through cooperative learning* (pp. 101–119). New York: Teachers College Press.

Stenmark, J. K., Thompson, V., & Cossey, R. (1987). *Family math.* Berkeley: Lawrence Hall of Science.

Sternberg, R. J. (1985). *Beyond IQ: A triarchic theory of human intelligence.* Cambridge, England: Cambridge University Press.

Tammivaara, J. (1982). The effects of task structure on beliefs about competence and participation in small groups. *Sociology of Education, 55,* 212–222.

Tudge, J. (1990). Vygotsky: The zone of proximal development and peer collaboration: Implications for classroom practice. In L. Moll (Ed.), *Vygotsky and education: Instructional implications and applications of sociohistorical psychology.* New York: Columbia University Press.

Webb, N. (1983). Predicting learning from student interaction: Defining the interaction variable. *Educational Psychologist, 18,* 33–41.

Webb, N. (1991). Task-related verbal interaction in mathematics learning in small groups. *Journal for Research in Mathematics Education, 22,* 366–389.

Webb, N., Ender, P., & Lewis, S. (1986). Problem-solving strategies and group processes in small groups learning computer programming. *American Educational Research Journal, 23,* 243–251.

Wilcox, M. (1972). *Comparison of elementary school children's interaction in teacher-led and student-led small groups.* Unpublished doctoral dissertation, Stanford University, Stanford, CA.

Yager, S., Johnson, D., & Johnson, R. (1985). Oral discussion, group-to-individual transfer and achievement in cooperative learning groups. *Journal of Educational Psychology, 77,* 60–66.

Zack, M. (1988, July). *Delegation of authority and the use of the student facilitator role.* Paper presented at the triannual meeting of the International Association for the Study of Cooperation in Education, Shefayim, Israel.

Index

About the Author

Elizabeth G. Cohen is Professor of Education and Sociology at Stanford University. Since 1968 she has carried out research on improving competence expectations of low-status youth. Her work began in the laboratory, but extended fo desegregated and multilingual schools. She has written widely on the subjects of cooperative learning, team teaching, the isolation of the teacher, and collegial evaluation.

Since 1982 she has directed the Program for Complex Instruction. With Dr. Rachel Lotan she has worked successfully with hundreds of elementary and middle school teachers in implementing activity-based classrooms for academically, ethnically, and linguistically heterogeneous populations.

ANNOUNCING A NEW VIDEO BY ELIZABETH COHEN!

Status Treatments for the Classroom

Elizabeth Cohen's own narrative in this video explains the origin of status problems and the rationale for these treatments. Accompanied by a pamphlet outlining how to use the video most effectively, *Status Treatments for the Classroom* will be an important tool—both standing alone and in tandem with *Designing Groupwork, Second Edition*—for pre- and inservice teachers, teacher educators, and staff developers interested in enhancing their use of the proven technique of cooperative learning in today's richly diverse classrooms.

1994/27-min. VHS/$55.00/ISBN 0-8077-3352-0

Please send me _____ copies of
Status Treatments for the Classroom @ $55.00 = Subtotal _____ .

- All personal orders must be prepaid or charged on credit card
- Purchase order must accompany institutional orders
- Prices subject to change without notice
- In Canada, order from: Guidance Centre, 712 Gordon Baker Road, Toronto, Ontario M2H 3R7

Tax (NY & VT residents only) _____

Postage & handling/first video __$2.50_____

$.75/each additional video _____

TOTAL __$_____

Name _____
(please print or type)

Address _____

_____

City _____ State _____ Zip _____

Daytime Tel. #: Area Code (_____) _____

Credit Card Orders: ☐ VISA ®. ☐ MasterCard ®.   Exp. Date _____

Card # _____

Signature _____
(no credit card orders accepted without signature)